D0146684

Bipolar Children

DISCARD

Recent Titles in
Childhood in America
Sharna Olfman, Series Editor

All Work and No Play . . . : How Educational Reforms
Are Harming Our Preschoolers
Sharna Olfman, Editor

Childhood Lost: How American Culture Is Failling Our Kids
Sharna Olfman, Editor

No Child Left Different
Sharna Olfman, Editor

The Last Normal Child: Essays on the Intersection of Kids,
Culture, and Psychiatric Drugs
Lawrence H. Diller

Bipolar Children
Cutting-Edge Controversy, Insights, and Research

EDITED BY SHARNA OLFMAN

Childhood in America

PRAEGER

Westport, Connecticut
London

Library of Congress Cataloging-in-Publication Data

Bipolar children : cutting-edge controversy, insights, and research / edited by Sharna Olfman.
    p. ; cm. — (Childhood in America)
  Includes bibliographical references and index.
  ISBN 978–0–275–99730–4 (alk. paper)
    1. Manic-depressive illness in children—United States. 2. Manic-depressive illness in children—Chemotherapy—United States. 3. Pediatric psychopharmacology—United States—Evaluation. I. Olfman, Sharna. II. Series.
  [DNLM: 1. Bipolar Disorder—diagnosis—United States. 2. Bipolar Disorder—drug therapy—United States. 3. Bipolar Disorder—epidemiology—United States. 4. Antipsychotic Agents—adverse effects—United States. 5. Child—United States. 6. Disease Outbreaks—United States. WM 207 B6152 2007]
  RJ506.D4B52 2007
  618.92′895—dc22   2007029918

British Library Cataloguing in Publication Data is available.

Copyright © 2007 by Sharna Olfman

All rights reserved. No portion of this book may be reproduced, by any process or technique, without the express written consent of the publisher.

Library of Congress Catalog Card Number: 2007029918
ISBN-13: 978–0–275–99730–4

First published in 2007

Praeger Publishers, 88 Post Road West, Westport, CT 06881
An imprint of Greenwood Publishing Group, Inc.
www.praeger.com

Printed in the United States of America

∞

The paper used in this book complies with the Permanent Paper Standard issued by the National Information Standards Organization (Z39.48–1984).

10 9 8 7 6 5 4 3 2 1

*In memory of Maggie Burston: educator, advocate,
and friend of the oppressed*

Contents

Acknowledgments

I wish to express my deep appreciation to each of the contributors to this volume for their scholarship and for their advocacy on behalf of children's welfare. Point Park University generously hosted the 2008 Childhood and Society Symposium on bipolar children, which enabled several of the contributors to meet and share their work. Elizabeth Evans, Point Park's library director, gave generously of her time and expertise. Special thanks to my parents, Bess and Mitchell Olfman; to my children, Adam and Gavriela; and to my husband, Daniel, whose loving support is an invaluable source of inspiration.

1

Bipolar Children: Cutting-Edge Controversy

SHARNA OLFMAN

On December 13, 2006, 4-year-old Rebecca Riley died of a prescription drug overdose. At $2\frac{1}{2}$ years of age, she was diagnosed with both bipolar disorder (BD) and attention-deficit/hyperactivity disorder (ADHD) by a respected psychiatrist at a clinic affiliated with Tufts University, who prescribed three medications; Depakote, an anti-seizure drug, Clonidine, an anti-hypertensive, and Seroquel, an antipsychotic. These three drugs were in her system at the time of her death.[1]

Until recently, giving toddlers multiple psychiatric diagnoses and drug cocktails was unheard of. Bipolar disorder was considered to be a rare, devastating disease whose average age of onset was adolescence or early adulthood. But in the last two decades, the field of children's mental health has undergone a disturbing change. Multiple diagnoses and polypharmacy regimens for children have became the norm, and BD is being diagnosed in children (some as young as one year of age) routinely. Many of these "bipolar" children have already received a diagnosis of ADHD and/or depression, and their new drug prescriptions for bipolar disorder are often added to ones that they are already taking. Bipolar preschoolers are now being recruited for drug trials of antipsychotics.

Why has our approach to the causes and treatment of children's psychological disturbances—and to pediatric bipolar disorder in particular—changed so dramatically? One widely held view is that advances in medical technologies, such as genetic mapping and fMRI scans, have led to a more finely honed understanding of the genetic and neurological origins of mental illnesses, which prompted the development of new drugs that target the source of these illnesses with laser-like precision. It is also widely believed that we have recently learned to recognize the early signs and symptoms of BD as they manifest in children, which we failed to notice in the past. But research does not support these claims. To date there are no genetic markers or brain-imaging tests that can definitively diagnose BD. Psychiatric assessment is still based on taking a family history, observing patients' behaviors and moods, self-reports, and impressions of caregivers such as parents and teachers—albeit often in an increasingly hasty and superficial fashion. And the "new" classes of drugs that are being used to treat BD are—if anything—less rather than more specific. In fact, these so called new drugs are anticonvulsants, which were designed to treat epilepsy, and atypical antipsychotics, which were originally developed to treat schizophrenia. The anticonvulsants and antipsychotics have simply been rebranded by pharmaceutical companies as "mood stabilizers." Both classes of drugs are major tranquilizers, and therefore they have a calming effect on agitated or manic patients. But it is important to note that *they do not address an underlying disease process* in the way that an antibiotic does. They treat symptoms, not underlying causes. Moreover, their effects are generic, so that *anyone* who takes them will be tranquilized. Worse still, none of these drugs has been approved by the U.S. Food and Drug Administration (FDA) for the prevention or cure of bipolar illness.[2]

In January 2007, the American Academy of Child and Adolescent Psychiatry (AACAP), the governing body of child and adolescent psychiatrists in the United States, issued new practice parameters for the assessment and treatment of children and teens with bipolar disorder in order to address some of these misconceptions. The authors of the AACAP practice parameters state the following:

- "The evidence is not yet sufficient to conclude that most presentations of juvenile mania are continuous with the classic adult disorder."[3]
- "The validity of diagnosing bipolar disorder in preschool children has not been established."[4]
- "The U.S. Food and Drug Administration (FDA) [has been advised] to only extend medication treatment studies down to age ten years, given concerns about the challenge of accurate diagnosis in younger children."[5]
- "The short- and long-term safety of mood stabilizers and atypical antipsychotic agents . . . in young children has not been established. It is particularly important with preschoolers that intervention strategies address environmental, developmental, temperamental, and social factors that may relate to symptom presentation."[6]

- "There are no biological tests, [not even] imaging or genetic studies, that are helpful in making the diagnosis of a bipolar disorder."[7]

This book examines the astonishing rise in the diagnosis of bipolar disorder in childhood in the absence of any compelling evidence for either the validity of the diagnostic criteria currently used, or for the safety and efficacy of the drugs being prescribed to treat it. It is not an "anti-psychiatric" or "anti-medical model" treatise. After all, three of the authors contributing to this volume are medical doctors (two psychiatrists and a developmental pediatrician), and all prescribe psychotropic drugs in a judicious manner. None of us would deny that genetic, neurological, and hormonal factors play a role in some psychological disturbances. The contributors to this volume do not reject science. Quite the contrary, we insist that rigorous scientific standards that do not imperil children's safety be reinstated in the research and treatment arenas. In order to fully appreciate the conditions that set the pediatric bipolar epidemic in motion, it is useful to begin with a brief history of bipolar illness.

BIPOLAR DISORDER IN HISTORICAL PERSPECTIVE

Originally named "manic-depressive psychosis," bipolar disorder was the first psychiatric illness to be identified by Emile Kraepelin—known as the father of modern psychiatry—in 1896. After a century of research on bipolar illness, Kraepelin's original descriptions of its symptoms and course have proven to be remarkably robust.[8] The international medical community still believes, as did Kraepelin, that BD is a devastating, albeit rare, genetically influenced brain disorder that begins in late adolescence or early adulthood, and is characterized by intense cycles of mania and depression. Outside of the United States, bipolar disorder is diagnosed less frequently than schizophrenia, itself an uncommon disorder.[9]

Symptoms typical of mania include marked euphoria, grandiosity, irritability, racing thoughts, increased psychomotor activity, rapidly shifting mood, and sleep disturbance. Paranoia, confusion, and psychosis are also typical. Depressive episodes are characterized by psychomotor retardation, oversleeping, suicide attempts, and often psychosis. Left untreated, the crashing lows and manic highs that are the hallmark of BD can ruin the lives of individuals and families.[10] Fortunately, in the mid-twentieth century Australian psychiatrist John Cade discovered that lithium carbonate not only had a calming effect on manic episodes, but also seemed to prevent future cycles of depression and mania. Although considered old-school by many practitioners, lithium carbonate remains the only drug that is recognized by the FDA to have a prophylactic effect on bipolar illness.

Approaches to diagnosis and treatment of BD in the United States began to diverge from those accepted in the rest of the world with the publication of the 1987 edition of the *Diagnostic and Statistical Manual of Mental Disorders* (*DSM-III-R*), the preeminent American system of psychiatric diagnosis. This version of the *DSM* introduced BD subtypes, which both broadened and diluted the criteria for diagnosing the disorder. The most current edition, the *DSM-IV-TR* (published in 2000), includes the following bipolar disorder subtypes:

- Bipolar 1 disorder with manic episode: Diagnosis requires one full-blown manic episode that lasts a minimum of seven days, although depression is not a requisite part of the symptom picture.
- Bipolar 2 disorder: Diagnosis is based on periods of major depression and at least one episode of "hypomania," a less intense form of mania that need be present for only four days.
- "Rapid-cycling" bipolar disorder: Diagnosis is based on the occurrence of at least four mood episodes per year.
- Bipolar disorder NOS (not otherwise specified): This diagnosis is given to patients whose symptoms do not meet the criteria for other bipolar diagnoses.

After bipolar subtypes were introduced into the *DSM* classification system, the number of U.S. adults meeting these much broader criteria began to soar. It is important to note that the World Health Organization, which publishes the *International Statistical Classification of Diseases and Related Health Problems*, now in its tenth edition (*ICD*-10), has more stringent diagnostic criteria for BD, which remains a rare disorder of adulthood.[11]

In the mid-1990s two child psychiatry research groups—one at Harvard, another at Washington University—began to train their attention on pediatric bipolar disorder. Both groups contend that until recently, bipolar disorder was underdiagnosed in children because the early symptoms of the illness are typically different from those in the adult phase. Both groups stress that a majority of bipolar children also suffer from ADHD, and that many were erroneously diagnosed with depression. The Washington group, headed by Barbara Geller, claims that children with bipolar illness often cycle through manic episodes that may last from a few minutes to a few days, as compared to manic episodes in adults that generally continue for several weeks or months if left untreated. Geller refers to brief, frequent manic episodes lasting from a few hours to less than four days as *ultrarapid cycling*, and she calls repeated brief daily cycles that last from minutes to hours *ultra-*

dian cycling. The Harvard group, led by Joseph Biederman, claims that bipolar children may not exhibit cyclic mood disturbances at all. Instead, they assert that these children may be chronically irritable and explosive, or chronically depressed and angry. Biederman's group has conducted several antipsychotic drug trials with bipolar preschoolers. As a result of Biederman and Geller's research, the diagnostic criteria for pediatric BD now extend to children who have brief stormy episodes of "mania" lasting only minutes, and to extremely moody, irritable, aggressive, or emotionally explosive children whose symptoms have almost no continuity with the *DSM* criteria, which are themselves much less stringent than the *ICD*-10 criteria.[12]

FROM THEORY TO PRACTICE

Claims by Geller and Biederman, that bipolar disorder often begins in childhood but with a different symptom picture, set the stage for the dramatic rise in the diagnosis of pediatric BD. But the diffusion of their ideas was greatly accelerated by a series of books written for the general public, the establishment of Web sites devoted to information about BD (which are heavily funded by drug companies), and the proliferation of bipolar drug ads targeted to consumers. In these materials, pediatric bipolar symptoms are stretched even further to include mildly irritable kids; preschoolers prone to temper tantrums; and creative, jubilant, high-energy children, many of whom have ended up on antipsychotics after a quick visit to the pediatrician.

The 2007 AACAP practice parameters represent an effort to stem these reckless diagnostic and prescribing practices by elucidating the differences between tentative research findings and sound clinical practice. However, despite the authors' honorable intentions, their recommendations scarcely address the many troubling questions that they themselves raise. The preamble to the AACAP practice parameters clearly states that there is no evidence to date that children exhibiting anything other than the classic symptoms of bipolar illness will in fact become bipolar adults. Yet the parameters also recommend that children with symptoms such as those identified by Biederman— which bear only a remote resemblance to the criteria for BD described in the *DSM*—be labeled "bipolar disorder NOS," without providing a cogent rationale for doing so. Unfortunately, whatever the theoretical rationale for a move like this might be, adding the caveat "not otherwise specified" to a diagnosis of BD will have almost no impact in terms of how an ostensibly bipolar child is regarded and treated by her parents, her teachers, and her physician, who will prescribe accordingly. The reason this is troubling is that the AACAP authors also state that the safety of atypical antipsychotic and anticonvulsant drugs has not been established with children, and yet, antipsychotic and anticonvulsant drugs are listed as first-line treatments for children diagnosed with bipolar 1 disorder. Finally, although they assert that there is no reliable method for diagnosing BD in preschool children, the authors do not recommend a moratorium on this practice and instead merely counsel caution.

Of even greater concern is the way in which the AACAP's practice parameters become diluted as they filter down—from clinicians working in university-affiliated clinics to psychiatrists in private practice; to pediatricians with no training in psychiatry or psychology; to harried, sleep-deprived residents and interns, who treat the vast majority of disadvantaged children. As a consequence, in the span of a decade, there has been a greater than fourfold increase in the number of children being diagnosed with BD—a trend that is exclusive to the United States. The majority of diagnosed children are being prescribed antipsychotic drugs, often in combination with anticonvulsant drugs. These classes of drugs have dangerous side effects that have led to a doubled mortality rate, shortened lifespan, extreme weight gain, and occurrence of type 2 diabetes.[13]

PEDIATRIC DEPRESSION AND THE SSRIs: A CAUTIONARY TALE ABOUT CONFLICT OF INTEREST

Whereas ADHD, with its attendant stimulant prescriptions, was the "darling" of child psychiatry in the 1980s, pediatric depression became the "diagnosis du jour" in the 1990s, leading to a steep rise in the prescription of SSRI[14] antidepressants such as Prozac to children and teens. Several years ago, psychiatrist David Healy, an international expert on mood disorders, discovered that the pharmaceutical industry was suppressing research demonstrating that SSRI antidepressants place children and adolescents at greater risk for suicidal and violent behavior. As a consequence of Healy's advocacy, SSRI antidepressants are now banned for use as first-line treatment for children in the United Kingdom. (An exception to the ban is Prozac, which can still be prescribed, but only after other interventions, such as psychotherapy, have been tried.) Healy's advocacy also influenced the October 2004 decision by the FDA that required all SSRI antidepressant prescriptions for children and adolescents to be issued with black-box warnings on package inserts stating that these drugs are known to increase the risk of suicidality in children. Requiring a black-box warning is the most stringent measure the FDA takes, short of removing a drug from the market.

Immediately following the FDA's ruling, the AACAP published comprehensive review articles that counseled caution in the use of antidepressant medications with children, but at the same time issued several statements and news releases urging psychiatrists to continue prescribing SSRIs for childhood depression. As a result there was a brief lull in SSRI sales immediately following the FDA decision, but antidepressant drug prescriptions to children are again proceeding apace.[15]

In the wake of his findings, Healy curtailed his ties with the pharmaceutical industry and lobbied vigorously to redress the conflicts of interest between the pharmaceutical industry and medical research. Unless the authors of medical treatment guidelines become completely free of drug company ties, they will be deterred from making treatment recommendations that undermine the market share of the companies that fund their research and pay their salaries.

The AACAP bipolar practice parameters document disclosed that two of its three authors had ties to the pharmaceutical industry. Lead author Robert McClellan received a research grant from Pfizer, and Robert Findling received research support, consulted with, and served on the speakers' bureaus of no fewer than sixteen pharmaceutical companies (Abbott, AstraZeneca, Bristol-Myers Squibb, Celltech-Medeva, Forest, Glaxo SmithKline, Johnson & Johnson, Lilly, New River, Novartis, Otsuka, Pfizer, Sanofi-Aventis, Shire, Solvaty, and Wyeth). As in the case of pediatric depression and the SSRIs, mental health practitioners will merely give lip service in their efforts to stem reckless diagnostic and prescription practices as long as profit-driven drug companies continue to fund the research on pediatric bipolar disorder. In light of the dire consequences for millions of children affected by irresponsible polypharmacy, these conflicts of interest are more than just misguided— they are completely immoral and should be made illegal.

THE PEDIATRIC BIPOLAR EPIDEMIC
IN CULTURAL CONTEXT

Questionable diagnostic and prescribing practices, fueled in large part by unethical partnerships between the medical profession and the pharmaceutical industry, are the direct cause of the American pediatric bipolar epidemic, but broad cultural trends have acted as enablers. These include the glaring absence of support for families in this nation, and society's faith in the "technological fix."

Families under Siege

One cultural condition that set the stage for the steep rise in child psychiatric diagnoses in general—and diagnoses of bipolar disorder in particular—is the dearth of public policy that supports the welfare of U.S. children and families. As expressed by Urie Bronfenbrenner, one of the finest developmental psychologists of the twentieth century: "The heart of our social system is the family. If we are to maintain the health of our society, we must discover the best means of nurturing that heart."[16] Tragically though, as Bronfenbrenner noted toward the end of his career, "the comparative lack of family support systems in the United States is so extreme as to make it unique among modern nations."[17]

How can a mother who must return to work only days after giving birth—while placing her newborn in substandard care—establish a secure attachment with her infant? If a single mother must work two or three low-wage jobs to make ends meet while her children return to an empty home, how can she scaffold their arduous journey toward adulthood? And how can she protect them from the tidal wave of violence, hatred, racism, sexism, and pornography that pervades the media? And if this mother is the second or third generation to have raised children under these compromised circumstances, how will she herself have acquired the psychological maturity and wisdom to relate lovingly and responsibly to her children? But these are precisely the conditions under which millions of American parents are obligated to raise their children. And when parents are overwhelmed, their children are more likely to be overwhelmed and overwhelming. Parents in turn become more reliant on and more vulnerable to the current climate in child psychiatry that views virtually all forms of psychological distress as a medical illness to be treated with drugs.

Mind as Machine Medicine

The medical model of mental illness conceptualizes psychological distress as symptomatic of an underlying medical condition. So, for example, just as fever may signify the presence of a virus, depression and mania are assumed to point to the presence of a genetically influenced brain disorder. This model makes an important contribution to the mental health field because it recognizes that genetic predisposition and brain anomalies can play a role in psychological disturbance. However, other models are equally essential to understanding the cause and cure of mental illness because they elucidate the role of social and cultural forces and the human condition in all of its rich complexity. The field of developmental psychology also offers vital insights, because it provides a yardstick of healthy development against which to measure disturbance. In addition, child development research sheds light on the complex and inextricable interplay of genes and environment that together shape brain development.

The medical model of mental disorders has monopolized the mental health field in recent decades, however, effectively "muscling out" other approaches and leading to a biased and distorted understanding of the cause and cure of psychological disturbance. The medical model holds so much sway in psychiatry, in part because it resonates so well with America's deep faith in technologies and the technological fix. The medical model lends itself to a conceptualization of the human mind as a machine whose software is a set of genes that we are learning to decode and recode, and whose hardware can be corrected or enhanced pharmacologically. Society has bought into the "mind as machine" metaphor to the extent that even children's expressions of emotion are being translated into the language of symptoms in need of pharmacological overhaul, as opposed to being accepted as meaningful communication. So, for example, a child's jubilant elation is reframed as "hypomania" and her sadness is termed "depression."

Learning to Feel

Emotions are not simple reflexes or instincts that are present in their mature form at birth and that are either in working order or in need of an "adjustment." Like other lines of development—such as intellectual, language, personality, and social development—emotional development follows a trajectory that is powerfully shaped by experience. In the early months and years, healthy emotional development depends on loving and consistent attachment to parents and other caregivers. As psychologist Robert Karen explains in *Becoming Attached*:

> The concept of "attachment", born in British psychoanalysis some forty years ago and nurtured to near maturity in the developmental psychology departments of American universities . . . encompasses both the quality and strength of the parent-child bond, the ways in which it forms and develops, how it can be damaged and repaired, and the long-term impact of separations, losses, wounds, and deprivations. Beyond that, *it is a theory of love and its central place in human life.*[18]

The attachment relationship teaches the infant to modulate, interpret, and communicate emotions. Sue Gerhardt describes this process in *Why Love Matters: How Affection Shapes a Baby's Brain*:

> To become fully human, the baby's basic responses need to be elaborated and developed into more specific and complex feelings. With parental guidance, the basic state of "feeling bad" can get differentiated into a range of feelings like irritation, disappointment, anger, annoyance

and hurt. . . . [T]he baby or toddler can't make these distinctions without help from those in the know. The parent must also help the baby to become aware of his own feelings and this is done by holding up a virtual mirror to the baby, talking in baby talk and emphasizing and exaggerating words and gestures so that the baby can realize that this is not mum or dad just expressing themselves, this is them "showing" me my feelings. It is a kind of "psychofeedback" which provides the introduction to a human culture in which we can interpret both our own and others' feelings and thoughts. Parents bring the baby into this more sophisticated emotional world by identifying feelings and labeling them clearly. Usually this teaching happens quite unselfconsciously.[19]

As Toni Vaughn Heineman discusses in Chapter 6, when a child is deprived of consistent and loving care in the first months and years of life, her emotional development will be stunted. For such a child, everything from mild disappointment to profound loss may engender rage, and everything from a simple courtesy to passionate love may elicit elation. Conversely an emotionally deprived child might defensively blunt all emotionally loaded experiences. We can imagine how in the current climate, derailed emotional development might be recast as early onset bipolar disorder.

EMOTIONS AND THE HUMAN CONDITION

When children's emotions—their highs and lows, anger and frustration, humiliation, irritation, giddiness, joy, and enthusiasm—are stripped of meaning and read exclusively as "symptoms," the consequences are profound. One of the most established theories to emerge from the discipline of social psychology is attribution theory. Simply put, when we attribute our behavior and our choices to forces beyond our control, we are much less likely to make an effort to modulate our behavior in the future. For example, if a child feels that her poor math score is attributable to her lack of talent in mathematics, then she is more likely to zone out, not do her homework, and not study very hard for her tests. By contrast, if she believes she has the potential to achieve excellent results, this will increase the likelihood that she will intensify her efforts in future. Similarly, when a young child is told by her parents and her doctor that, for example, her rudeness, tantrums, or flippant remarks are symptoms of an illness, then she and they will think that she is incapable of modulating her behavior without a drug intervention, and this effectively will cut off the process of emotional development by short-circuiting opportunities for life lessons and personal accountability. When emotional expression is stripped of meaning, then a deeply troubling or traumatic experience may remain unearthed, and the child may be taught, in effect, to tune out her feelings as well as those of others.

When a form of experience and expression that is integral to our humanity and essential to our full engagement with life is reduced to a symptom, then we are *dehumanizing* our children and treating them like machines to be programmed rather than as children to be loved, taught, mentored, and disciplined. We do this in the name of science, and for the sake of our own convenience and peace of mind. But in so doing, we undermine our children's capacity to experience life fully and to empathize with others, and we curtail their chances of experiencing genuine intimacy and of forming stable and sustaining personal relationships with others. In short, we compound the systemic problems that gave rise to our children's problems in the first place!

STEMMING THE TIDE OF THE PEDIATRIC BIPOLAR TSUNAMI

Many of the children and adolescents who have been *labeled* with BD, now numbering in the millions, are in great emotional pain, and in some cases they are an overwhelming challenge to their families. But in the vast majority of cases, they are not suffering from BD. A child who is misdiagnosed with a bipolar illness is effectively denied treatment for the real source of her suffering. And when we expand and distort the diagnostic criteria for BD beyond recognition, we risk making a mockery of a grave illness, and may deny those who do suffer from it access to effective research and treatment. When a child is unnecessarily prescribed antipsychotic and anticonvulsant drugs, her mental and physical health may be irrevocably compromised. With as many as two and a half million children from across the socioeconomic spectrum now taking antipsychotics, we have set the stage for wide-scale child abuse. We must stem this tide of misdiagnoses and dangerous drug prescriptions. Together, the contributors to this book identify the complex and interrelated factors that have set the stage for the pediatric bipolar epidemic in order to raise awareness and recommend practice and policy changes.

2

Bipolar Syndrome by Proxy?: The Case of Pediatric Bipolar Disorder

DAVID HEALY AND JOANNA LE NOURY

BACKGROUND

The Marketing of Bipolar Disorder

In the same way that other corporations selling everything from sportswear to automobiles research the needs of their market, pharmaceutical companies attempt to establish the unmet needs of their market.[1] As other companies do, pharmaceutical companies use focus groups. For drug companies, focus groups consist of physicians, or in the case of psychotropic drugs, psychiatrists. From groups like these that included opinion leaders in psychiatry, it was discovered some years ago that a series of unmet mental health needs clustered around the concept of bipolar disorder. The field—that is, other psychiatrists, mental health workers, and the public—were prepared to believe that bipolar disorder could affect up to 5 percent of the population; that it was an unacknowledged and underresearched disorder; that antidepressants might not be good for this disorder; that the disorder might be better treated with a mood stabilizer; and that everybody stood to gain by encouraging a process of patient self-monitoring.

Early focus-group and related marketing research on bipolar disorder coincided with the introduction of Depakote as a mood stabilizer. This anticonvulsant drug, which had been available in the form of sodium valproate since the mid-1960s and had then been shown to be potentially helpful in manic-depressive illness by French and later by German groups, was reformulated by Abbott

Laboratories in the form of a semi-sodium valproate salt.[2] Abbott claimed that this salt, infinitesimally different from its parent compound, formed a more stable solution than sodium valproate. The trivial distinction between the two was nevertheless sufficient to enable the company to take a patent out on the new compound. The new compound was named Depakote and introduced in 1995 for the treatment of mania, after approval by the Food and Drugs Administration (FDA) on the basis of trials that showed that this very sedative agent could produce beneficial effects in the treatment of acute manic states.[3] However, it is important to note that any sedative agent can produce some demonstrable benefits in the treatment of acute manic states. No company had chosen to do so until then because manic states were comparatively rare and were adequately controlled by available treatments.

Almost from the start, Depakote was advertised as a mood stabilizer. If it had been advertised as prophylactic for manic-depressive disorder, the FDA would have had to rule the ad illegal because a prophylactic effect for valproate in manic-depressive disease had not been demonstrated to the standards required for licensing. The term "mood stabilizer," by contrast, was until then a rarely used term that had no precise clinical or neuroscientific meaning.[4] As such it was not open to legal sanction. It was a new brand. Depakote quickly gained a reputation as a mood stabilizer even though more than a decade has passed and still no studies have proven that it is effective in treating manic-depressive illness. Despite the fact that the term still has no precise clinical or neuroscientific meaning, mood stabilizers are widely used, and a range of other anticonvulsant and antipsychotic drugs—such as olanzapine, quetiapine, and risperidone—are now identified as mood stabilizers. Before 1995 there were almost no articles in the medical literature on mood stabilizers; now more than a hundred a year are published.[5]

Both clinicians and patients have been happy to endorse the rebranding of sedatives as mood stabilizers, despite a continuing lack of evidence that these drugs are effective for this purpose. In addition to branding a new class of psychotropic drugs, the 1990s saw the rebranding of an old illness. Manic-depressive illness became bipolar disorder. As late as 1990, the leading book on this disease was called *Manic-Depressive Disease*,[6] but it is rare to hear the term today. This combination of a brand-new disease and brand-new drug class was historically unprecedented in psychiatry, and the clashing of these tectonic plates unleashed a tidal wave of marketing designed to convince physicians and the public of the prevalence of bipolar disorder and calling for the prescription of mood stabilizers.

The Marketing of "Mood Stabilizers"

The original mood stabilizers were Depakote and a series of anti-convulsant drugs. But antipsychotic drugs were drawn irresistibly into the feeding frenzy. Lilly, Janssen, and Astra-Zeneca, the makers of olanzapine (Zyprexa), risperidone (Risperdal), and quetiapine (Seroquel), respectively, have sought to have these drugs recognized as mood stabilizers, and the steps they have taken to market their compounds illustrate a great deal about how companies go about creating markets. We will outline five such steps.

Step 1: Patient Literature

Each of the companies has produced patient literature and Web-site materials aimed at teaching people about bipolar disorder. This process involves diseasemongering.[7] Patients are supposedly being educated about the disease as a way to sell medication. In the case of Zyprexa, patient leaflets and booklets routed through patient groups state that bipolar disorder is a lifelong illness requiring lifelong treatment; that symptoms come and go but that the illness stays; that people feel better because the medication is working; that almost everyone who stops taking the medication will become ill again; and that the more episodes one experiences, the more difficult they are to treat.[8] This is almost precisely the same message found in Janssen Pharmaceuticals' self-help guide for people with bipolar disorder. Under the heading "The Right Medicine at the Right Time," the leaflet states: "Medicines are crucially important in the treatment of bipolar disorders. Studies over the past twenty years have shown without a shadow of doubt that people who have received the appropriate drugs are better off in the long term than those who receive no medicine."[9]

If studies had actually shown this over the past twenty years, a number of drugs would have been licensed for the prevention of bipolar disorder, but in fact no drugs had been licensed until recently. Lithium was the only drug that had produced demonstrable evidence for prophylactic efficacy, but not even lithium was licensed by the FDA. Even more troubling are the extremely dangerous side effects of antipsychotic and anticonvulsant drugs. All studies of life expectancy of patients taking antipsychotics show a doubling of mortality rates compared to control groups, and this doubling increases again for every added antipsychotic drug the patient takes.[10] Patients on antipsychotics also have reduced life expectancy.[11] In addition, all studies to date on the treatment of bipolar disorder with mood stabilizers such as Depakote, Zyprexa, and Risperdal show that suicide risk doubles, compared to treatment with placebo.[12] Valproate and other anticonvulsant mood stabilizers are among the most teratogenic (damaging to fetal development) drugs in medicine.[13] Statements about the benefits of treatment are therefore more than just misleading—they are duplicitous. This brings out a point about the relationship between pharmaceutical companies and patient groups. No company could readily make such statements without the regulators' intervention. By using patient groups or academics, companies can palm off the legal liability for such statements.[14]

Step 2: Famous Manic-Depressives

Another ploy commonly used in marketing mood-stabilizing drugs is the creation of lists of writers, poets, playwrights, artists, and composers who have supposedly suffered from bipolar disorder. Material from Kay Jamison's book *Touched with Fire* has been widely reproduced.[15] To look at some of these lists, you would think that most of the major artists of the nineteenth and twentieth centuries had experienced bipolar disorder, when in fact very few if any of the persons listed had a confirmed diagnosis of manic-depressive illness.

Step 3: Mood Diaries

Mood diaries are another mechanism for promoting these drugs. The diaries break up the day into hourly segments and ask people to rate their moods on a scale that typically goes from 15 to 25. For example, on the Lilly-sponsored mood diary,[16] you rate a 12 if you are very productive (i.e., doing things to excess such as making phone calls, writing, having tea, smoking, being charming, and being talkative). For a score of 11, your self-esteem is judged to be good, and you are considered to be optimistic, sociable, articulate, decisive, and productive. A score of 21 involves slight withdrawal from social situations, having less concentration than usual, and perhaps feeling slight agitation. A score of 22 involves feelings of panic and anxiety with poor concentration and memory and some discomfort in routine activities. Most normal people during the course of a week probably cycle between at least 12 and 22, which is almost precisely the point behind this mood watching. Most normal people show a bipolar variation in their moods—an incipient bipolar mood disorder.

Step 4: Questionnaires

On the Web site IsItReallyDepression.com[17] Astra-Zeneca provides a mood questionnaire that asks, among other things, whether there has been a period of time when you were more irritable than usual, more self-confident than usual, got less sleep than usual and found you didn't really miss it, were more talkative than usual, had thoughts race through your mind, had more energy than usual, were more active than usual, were more social or outgoing than usual, or had more libido than usual. These are all functions that show some variation in every normal person. Answering yes to seven of these questions leads to two further questions: Whether you have ever engaged in more than one of these behaviors at any one time, and whether you have ended up in some sort of trouble as a result of this behavior. If you answer yes to these two questions, you may meet criteria for bipolar disorder and are advised to seek a review by a mental health professional. Whether or not you meet these criteria, if you are concerned, it is suggested that you might want to seek a mental health assessment anyway. The Web site and ads indicate that people often miss the diagnosis of bipolar disorder because when they are depressed they are so focused on their depression that they are unable to remember their manic symptoms. Or they only seek help when depressed. Or they are misled by the high public awareness of depression and neglect of mania. It apparently often requires a professional third party to spot your manic features or periods.

This measurement-induced mood watching has a parallel in the new behavior of weight watching that came with the introduction of weight scales.[18] This new behavior coincided with the emergence of eating disorders in the 1870s. An even greater increase in frequency of eating disorders in the 1920s ran parallel to a much wider public availability of weight scales and the emergence of norms for weight that had an almost immediate impact on societal ideas of what is beautiful and healthy. In the 1960s there was an explosion of eating disorders that again occurred in parallel with the development of smaller bathroom scales now common in almost every home. What we see here is the power of measurement—how figures from one area of our lives can come to dominate our lives.

There is an informational reductionism here that is perhaps even more potent than the biological reductionism pointed to by many critics of modern psychiatry. Measuring is not inherently a problem and figures may provide potent reinforcement, but the abstraction that is measurement can lead to an oversight for context and for other dimensions of an individual's functioning or situation that are not open to measurement or that are simply not being measured. If this happens, we are not being modestly scientific by measuring what we can—we are being pseudoscientific.

Step 5: Marketing Risk

The fifth strategy involves marketing risk. These tactics have been used in the promotion of drugs for a variety of illnesses, including depression, osteoporosis, hypertension, and others. In the case of osteoporosis, companies may present images of a top model in her mid-twenties and looking her best, juxtaposed with a computer-generated image of the same woman as she might look in her mid-sixties or -seventies and suffering severe osteoporosis. On the one hand we see a beautiful woman; on the other, we see a shrunken crone. The message is that "you can never be too safe." If one wants to retain beauty and vitality, it is best to start treatment early. In the case of mood disorders, the risks being marketed are the risks of suicide, alcoholism, divorce, career failure, and so on.

This strategy was used to great effect in a now famous direct-to-consumer ad produced by Lilly, the maker of Zyprexa (olanzapine). It begins with a vibrant woman dancing late into the night. A background voice says: "Your doctor never sees you like this." The ad cuts to a shrunken and glum figure, and the voiceover now says: "This is who your doctor sees." Cutting again to the woman in active shopping mode, clutching bags with the latest brand names, we hear "This is why so many people who have bipolar disorder are being treated for depression and aren't getting any better—because depression is only half the story." We see the woman depressed, looking at bills that have arrived in the mail, and then we see her again, energetically painting her apartment. "That fast-talking, energetic, quick-tempered, up-all-night you," says the voiceover, "probably never shows up in the doctor's office." No drugs are mentioned. But viewers are encouraged to log onto bipolarawareness.com, which links to a Web site called "Bipolar Help Center," sponsored by Lilly Pharmaceuticals, the maker of olanzapine (Zyprexa). The Web site contains a "mood disorder questionnaire."[19] In the television ad, we see our heroine logging onto bipolarawareness.com and finding this questionnaire. The voice encourages the viewer to follow the woman's example: "Take the test you can take to your doctor; it can change your life. Getting a correct diagnosis is the first step in helping your doctor to help you."

This ad can be read as a genuine attempt to alert people who may be suffering from one of the most debilitating and serious psychiatric diseases—manic-depressive illness. Alternatively, it can be read as an example of what has been termed diseasemongering. Whichever it is, it reaches beyond those suffering from a mood disorder to others who will now be more likely to see their personal experiences in a new way, and will lead to medical consultations and may shape the outcome of those consultations. Ads that encourage "mood watching" risk misreading the variations on an emotional even keel as indicators of latent or actual bipolar disorder. The ad described appeared in 2002, shortly after Lilly's antipsychotic olanzapine was licensed for treating mania. The company was at the time also running trials aimed at establishing olanzapine as a mood stabilizer.

Bipolar Disorder and Mood Stabilizers: A Marketing Success

The upshot of the intensive efforts to increase the number of diagnoses of psychiatric illnesses and market their attendant drugs has been to dramatically alter the landscape of mental disorders. Until recently manic-depressive illness was a rare disorder in the United States, involving only ten per one million new cases each year, or 3,000 new cases per year at the current level of population. The disorder occurred eight times less frequently than schizophrenia. In contrast, bipolar disorder is now thought to affect 5 percent of the people in the United States, or fifteen million Americans. It is now diagnosed as often as depression, and ten times more often than schizophrenia. Clinicians are encouraged to detect and treat it. They are being educated to suspect that many cases of depression, anxiety, or schizophrenia may in fact be bipolar disorder, and to adjust treatment accordingly.[20]

BIPOLAR DISORDER IN CHILDREN

The emergence of bipolar disorder in children must be reviewed against the background outlined above. Until very recently manic-depressive illness was not thought to start before the teenage years. Quite rarely it had its onset in early or middle puberty, but more often it started in the later pubertal years, with the most common ages of onset in the twenties and thirties. The clearest indicator of the changing picture with regard to juvenile bipolar disorder came with the publication in 2000 of *The Bipolar Child* by Papolos and Papolos.[21] This book sold 70,000 hardback copies in half a year. Published in January 2000, by May it was in its tenth printing. Other books followed, claiming that we are facing an epidemic of bipolar disorder in children[22] and that children should be treated aggressively with drugs from a young age to have any hope of a normal life.[23] And newspapers throughout the United States began to run stories about children with bipolar disorder.

A series of books aimed at children appeared. In *My Bipolar Roller Coaster Feelings Book* by Bryna Hebert,[24] a young boy named Robert tells us he has bipolar disorder. As Robert explains, doctors say you are bipolar if your feelings go to the top and bottom of the world like a roller coaster. When Robert is happy he apparently hugs everybody, starts giggling, and feels like doing backflips. His parents call it "bouncing off the walls." His doctor, Dr. Janet, describes it as being silly, giddy, and goofy. Aside from giddiness, Robert exhibits three other features that seem to confirm the diagnosis of bipolar disorder. The first is that he has temper tantrums. He is shown going into the grocery store with his mother and asking for candy. When she refuses he gets angry and throws the bag of candy at her. His mother calls this behavior "rage" and Robert is described as feeling bad afterward. The second telling feature is that Robert has nightmares when he goes to bed at night. His brain races like a movie in fast-forward, and he can't seem to stop it. The third feature is that at times he is just plain cranky. Everything irritates him—from the seams in his socks to his sister's voice and the smell of food cooking. This irritation can change into depression when he is sad and lonely. At these times he just wants to curl up in his bed and pull the blanket over his head. He feels as though it's the end of the world and no one cares about him. Dr. Janet has told him that at such times he needs to tell his parents or his doctor and he needs to get help.

Dr. Janet sorts Robert out with medication. Robert's view is that although he doesn't like having bipolar disorder, he can't change it. He also doesn't like having to take all those pills, but the bad nightmares have gone away and the medicine helps him have more good days. His father says a lot of kids have something wrong with their bodies, such as asthma or diabetes, and they have to take medicine and be careful, so from this point of view Robert is just like many other children. His parents have told him that his bipolar disorder is just a part of who he is, not *all* of who he is, and that they love him and always will. Finally, Dr. Janet is reported as saying that doctors haven't known for very long that children could have bipolar disorder, and that they are working hard to help these children feel better. The back of this book shows a collage of photographs featuring thirty to forty children and a question posed in the middle: "One out of five children has a diagnosable and treatable mental health need. Can you pick them out?"

Another book in this genre is *Brandon and the Bipolar Bear* by Tracy Anglada,[25] which introduces us to Brandon. Like Robert, Brandon has behaviors that many people might not see as indicative of bipolar disorder. When we are introduced to Brandon, he has just woken up from a nightmare—like Robert. He finally gets back to sleep, but then he is unable to get up the next morning. Like Robert, when Brandon is requested to do things he doesn't want to do, he flies into a rage. In his rage, he happens to destroy his bear. His mother offers to take both Brandon and the bear to Dr. Samuel for help. Brandon is thrilled and, like Robert, he responds by being silly, giddy, and goofy.

The exchange at the doctor's office involves Brandon being told that he has bipolar disorder. Dr. Samuel explains that the way we feel is controlled by chemicals in our brain. In people with bipolar disorder these chemicals can't do their job right so their feelings get jumbled inside. You might feel wonderfully happy, horribly angry, very excited, terribly sad, or extremely irritated, all in the same day. It's scary, and it can be so confusing that living can seem too hard. When Brandon wonders if he got bipolar disorder because he is bad, Dr. Samuel responds that many children just like him have bipolar disorder and they come to the doctor for help. Neither they nor Brandon are bad—they just have an illness that makes them feel bad. Dr. Samuel asks Brandon how he got his green eyes and brown hair. Brandon and his mother respond that these traits came from his parents. And Dr. Samuel tells them it's the same with bipolar disorder—it can be inherited, and someone else in the family may have it, too.

The final exchange involves Brandon asking whether he will ever feel better. Dr. Samuel responds in an upbeat manner that this is the good news—that there are good medicines to help people with bipolar disorder, and that Brandon can start by taking one right away. But Brandon must do two more things: he must promise to take his medicine when his mother tells him to, and he is asked to come back to see Dr. Samuel soon. *Brandon and the Bipolar Bear* comes with a coloring book. In the coloring book, a character called Dad makes it clear that a lot of kids have things wrong with their bodies, such as asthma and diabetes, and those kids also have to take medicine and be careful.

In a review on the back cover of *Brandon and the Bipolar Bear*, Janice Papolos, coauthor of *The Bipolar Child*, writes that "children will follow (and relate to) Brandon's experience with rapid mood swings, irritability, his sense of always being uncomfortable, and his sadness that he can't control himself and [that] no one can fix him. The comforting explanation that Dr Samuel gives him makes Brandon feel not alone, not bad, but hopeful that the medicine will make him feel better. We were so moved by the power of this little book and we feel better that we can now highly recommend a book for children aged 4 through 11."

The book *The Bipolar Child* arrived at Sheri Lee Norris's home in Hurst, Texas, in February 2000. When it did, Karen Brooks, a reporter for the *Dallas Star-Telegram*, describes her as tearing open the package with a familiar mix of emotions; hope, skepticism, fear, guilt, shame, and love. But as she reads in the book about violent rages, animal abuse, inability to feel pain, self-abuse, and erratic sleeping patterns,

Norris reportedly feels relief for the first time in more than a year. Now she finally knows what is wrong with her daughter. Within days Heather Norris, then two years old, became the youngest child in Tarrant County with a diagnosis of bipolar disorder, commonly known as manic depression.[26]

Brooks goes on to note that families with mentally ill children are plagued with insurance woes, lack of treatment options, and weak support systems, but that parents of the very young with mental illness face additional challenges. It is particularly hard to get the proper diagnosis and treatment because scant research has been done on childhood mental illnesses and drug treatments to combat them. Routine child care is difficult to find because day-care centers, worried about the effect on other children, won't accept mentally ill children or will remove them when they display aggressive behavior. Few babysitters have the expertise or the desire to handle difficult children. Parents often have little choice but to quit work or work from home.

Having outlined these difficulties, Brooks also notes that the lack of societal awareness of childhood mental illness means that parents are judged when their children behave badly. They are accused of being bad parents, or even of sexual or physical abuse, neglect, or failing to discipline their children properly. The sense of hopelessness is aggravated when parents hear about mentally ill adults; they wonder whether the battles they and their children are fighting will go on forever. In a few short paragraphs in her feature in the *Star Telegram*, Brooks outlines the once and future dynamics of disease, from ancient to modern times—its reflection on parents or family, the concerns for the future, the hope for an intervention. But she also covers a set of modern and specifically American dynamics that brought Heather Norris to this point.

Heather's problems began with temper tantrums when she was eighteen months old. Heather's mother was visited by a caseworker from the Child Protective Services. Someone she trusted had turned her in because Heather behaved abnormally. Norris was furious. She took Heather to pediatricians, play therapists, and psychiatrists, where Heather was diagnosed with ADHD and given Ritalin, which made everything worse. Faced with all this, a psychiatrist declined to diagnose bipolar disorder because the family had no history of it—or so Heather's mother thought. But she began asking relatives and discovered that mental illness was, indeed, in her family's history. She presented this information, along with a copy of *The Bipolar Child*, to her psychiatrist, and Heather was diagnosed with bipolar disorder immediately.

Heather Norris's story is not unusual. The epidemic of bipolar disorder diagnoses in children hit the cover of *Time* in August 2002. The magazine featured nine-year-old Ian Palmer with the cover title "Young and Bipolar"[27] and the subtitle "Why are so many kids being diagnosed with the disorder, once known as manic depression?" The *Time* piece and other articles like it stressed that surveys show that 20 percent of adolescents nationwide have some form of diagnosable mental disorder. Ian Palmer, we are told, like Heather Norris, had begun treatment early—at age three—but failed to respond to either Prozac or stimulants, and was now taking anticonvulsants. The issue of childhood bipolar disorder also hit the editorial columns of the *American Journal of Psychiatry* in 2002.[28]

In 2000 at age two, Heather Norris was the youngest child in Tarrant County to be diagnosed as bipolar. That same year, however, Papolos and Papolos found that many of the mothers they interviewed for *The Bipolar Child* remembered their baby's excessive activity in utero, and they seemed happy to make connections between such activity and their child's later diagnosis of bipolar disorder. Accounts of excessive activity referred to hard kicking, rolling, and tumbling by the fetus, and to keeping the ward awake with screaming as a new-born. In some instances mothers were told by their obstetrician that it was difficult to get a picture of the baby's face or to sample the amniotic fluid because of the baby's constant, unpredictable activity.[29] It is not unusual to meet clinicians who take such reports seriously.

Anyone searching the Internet for information on bipolar disorder in children is likely to end up at BPChildren.com, run by Tracy Anglada and several coauthors of the books mentioned above. Another frequent stop is the *Juvenile Bipolar Research Foundation* (JBRF) Web site, which links to the Papolos's Web site featuring their book, *The Bipolar Child*. Your search may also lead you to a third site, bpkids.org, which links to the site *Child and Adolescent Bipolar Foundation*. All three sites offer mood-watching questionnaires for children, similar to the mood-watching questionnaires common in the adult field. The *Juvenile Bipolar Research Foundation* Web site includes the sixty-five–item child bipolar questionnaire cited in the *Time* magazine piece. Most normal children taking the questionnaire would score at least moderately high.[30]

THE ACADEMIC VOICE

Until very recently manic-depressive illness was thought not to start before the teenage years. The standard view had been established in the early years of the twentieth century by Theodore Ziehen, who claimed (against some opposition) that it was possible, albeit unusual, for the illness to start during adolescence.[31] This was the accepted wisdom on this disorder for nearly one hundred years, and remains the accepted wisdom outside the United States. As of 2007 European articles continue to express doubt about the existence of prepubertal bipolar disorder.[32] The view in Europe is that patterns of overactivity can be seen in patients with learning disabilities, mental retardation, or Asperger's syndrome, but it is not clear that these symptoms should be regarded as evidence of manic-depressive illness.

In 1996 Barbara Geller and her colleagues in St. Louis framed the first set of criteria for possible bipolar disorder in children as part of a National Institute of Mental Health (NIMH)–funded study.[33] Using these criteria the first studies, which were reported in 2002, suggested that little was known about the condition. There were children who might meet the criteria, but these children had a very severe condition that in other circumstances would likely have been diagnosed as childhood schizophrenia, or they displayed patterns of overactivity against a background of mental retardation.[34]

However, Geller's research and the entire debate had been derailed by the time she reported her first study. In 1997 a paper from an influential Harvard-based group working in the ADHD field suggested that some pediatric patients who appear to have ADHD may in fact have mania or bipolar disorder.[35] Although the study relied on lay raters, failed to interview the children about themselves, used no prepubertal age-specific mania items, and used an instrument designed for studying the epidemiology of ADHD, its message stuck. Cases of bipolar disorder were being misdiagnosed as ADHD. Given the many children already in the treatment system who did not respond to stimulants, and given the clinicians who were casting around for another option, this was a potent message. A study by Peter Lewinsohn and colleagues in 2000 added fuel to the fire.[36] Even though this study primarily involved adolescents and pointed toward ill-defined overactivity rather than to proper bipolar disorder, the message it sent was that a greater frequency of bipolar disorder in minors existed than had been previously suspected.

These developments led to a 2001 NIMH roundtable meeting on prepubertal bipolar disorder[37] to discuss the issues further. By then, however, any meeting or publication—even one skeptical in tone—was likely to inflame the situation. To simply talk about pediatric bipolar disorder was to endorse it. Around this time the *Juvenile Bipolar Research Foundation* Web site noted that bipolar disorder in children simply does not look like bipolar disorder in adults in that children's moods swing several times a day—children do not experience several weeks or months of elevated mood, as adults do. This Web site baldly states that "the *DSM* needs to be updated to reflect what the illness looks like in childhood."[38] The Child and Adolescent Bipolar Foundation convened a meeting in July 2003 that was supported by unrestricted educational grants from Abbott, Astra-Zeneca, Eli Lilly, Forrest, Janssen, Novartis, and Pfizer. The participants initiated work on treatment guidelines that assumed the widespread existence of bipolar disorder and the need to map out treatment algorithms involving cocktails of multiple drugs.[39]

There are many contradictions here. The first is in the willingness to set aside all evidence from adult manic-depressive illness, which involves mood states persisting for weeks or months, and to argue that children's moods may oscillate rapidly, up to several times per day. At one and the same time, it is assumed that this disorder is continuous with the adult illness and should therefore (by extrapolation) be treated with the same drugs used for adults. Another contradiction that the framers of the U.S position fail to recognize is that the *DSM-IV-TR* is already much more liberal in its criteria for bipolar disorder when compared with international systems of classification. Ironically, advocates of pediatric bipolar disorder repeatedly point to problems with the *DSM-IV-TR* that hold them back from making diagnoses and treating children. In fact, the *DSM-IV-TR* is out of step with the rest of world in requiring a diagnosis of bipolar disorder following a manic episode. The *International Classification of Disease* permits a diagnosis of freestanding manic episodes—and indeed, permits several manic episodes—without a commitment to a diagnosis of bipolar disorder. The rest of the world believes it simply does not know enough about this relatively well-understood adult illness to achieve diagnostic consistency worldwide. The *DSM-IV-TR* already makes it much easier to diagnose bipolar disorder than any other classification system ever has.

Finally, we appear to have entered a world of operational criteria by proxy. Clinicians are not making these diagnoses based on openly visible signs in the patients in front of them as is traditional in medicine. Nor are they making the diagnoses based on what their patients say, as has been standard in adult psychiatry. Rather, these diagnoses are being made on the basis of what is said by such third parties as parents or teachers, without any assessment of the range of influences that might trigger parents or teachers to say such things—the range of influences brought out vividly by Karen Brooks in her *Star-Telegram* articles.

When clinicians raise just this point, as Boston's Jennifer Harris did in 2005,[40] the response has been aggressively dismissive as typified by Dilsaver's commentary:

> Mood need not be elevated, irritable, etc., for a week to fulfill criteria. . . . A period of four days suffices for hypomania. This is . . . itself an arbitrary figure under scrutiny . . . . Dr. Harris is incorrect [in stating] that the prevalence of adult bipolar disorder is only 1–2 percent. When all variants are considered the disease is likely to be present in more than 6 percent of the adult population. There are still those who will not accept that children commonly suffer from bipolar illness regardless of how weighty the evidence. One cannot help but wonder whether there are not political and economic reasons for this stubborn refusal to allow the outmoded way of thought articulated by Dr. Harris to die a peaceful death. It is a disservice to our patients to do otherwise.[41]

Although one might have thought some of the more distinguished institutions would weigh in with some healthy skepticism, they appear instead to be fueling the fire. Massachusetts General Hospital (MGH) has run trials of the antipsychotics risperidone and olanzapine on children with a mean age of four years.[42] A mean age of four all but guarantees that three- and possibly two-year-olds have been recruited to participate in these studies.

Massachusetts General in fact recruited juvenile subjects for these and other trials by running its own ads featuring clinicians and parents. The ads alerted parents that difficult and aggressive behavior in children from the age of four might stem from bipolar disorder. It is all but impossible for a short-term trial of sedative drugs *not* to significantly lessen activity levels in children, resulting in statistically significant rating-scale changes, and thereby confirming the apparent reality of juvenile bipolar disorder. As a result of trials such as these, dangerous drugs such as olanzapine and risperidone are now used extensively to treat U.S. children, including preschoolers, with relatively little questioning. In sharp contrast, it remains rare for clinicians elsewhere in the world to make a diagnosis of manic-depressive illness before patients reach their mid- to late teens.[43] It is now more attractive to pharmaceutical companies to fund academics to run drug trials on their behalf rather than to submit their data to the FDA in order to gain licensure for the treatment of children. Companies can then count on clinicians to follow academic researchers' recommendations, which are delivered at professional meetings or in published articles. As it stands, pharmaceutical companies have no need to submit data to the FDA or risk having lawyers and others pry through their archives to study the actual results of studies. As an additional benefit, academics "cost" a lot less than putting a sales force in the field.

NEW VARIANT OF MUNCHAUSEN'S SYNDROME?

As outlined above, a number of forces appear to have conspired to produce something of a tidal wave that has swept aside traditional defenses. This has led to an increasing number of children and infants being put on cocktails of some of the most toxic drugs in medicine with no evidence of actual prophylactic benefit. One of the interesting features of the story as it has unfolded is how so few players have been able to effect such an extraordinary change. Take, for example, the case of the academic Robert Post, who was among the first to propose that anticonvulsants might be useful for manic-depressive disease in adults. When the frequency of the disorder began to increase rather than decrease, Post began to promote the idea that the reason for this failure was that the affected individuals had not been caught early enough— and no age seemed too young. According to Post:

> One would encourage major efforts at earlier recognition and treatment of this potentially incapacitating and lethal recurrent central nervous system disorder. It would be hoped that instituting such early, effective, and sustained prophylactic intervention would not only lessen illness-related morbidity over this interval, but [would] also change the course of illness toward a better trajectory and more favorable prognosis.[44]

Another group consists of parents and clinicians who bring evangelical fervor to widening the bipolar disorder diagnosis. Some of these parents and clinicians readily contemplate the possibility of making a diagnosis in utero. In a climate in which those challenging such viewpoints are subject to opprobrium, it must be asked what has happened to the academic leaders that should be questioning exactly what is happening here. Finally, there are the companies that make available a range of psychoactive drugs, unrestricted educational grants, and access to academic platforms. These groups have clearly facilitated the epidemic of pediatric bipolar diagnoses.

If this process could reasonably be expected to lead to benefits, it could be regarded as therapeutic. But there is no evidence for benefit, and abundant prima facie evidence that giving such toxic drugs to such vulnerable subjects in such large quantities can only produce difficulties for many of these minors and infants. Are we witnessing a variation on Munchausen's syndrome, in which the patient, the parent, or some significant other wants the child to be ill and derives some gain from these proxy illnesses?

As a quick reality check, consider the following. Along with colleagues, the authors collected the North West Wales records of all admissions to the asylum in North Wales for the fifty-year period between 1875 and 1924. Among the close to 3,500 individuals admitted from a population base of slightly more than a quarter-million, only 123 individuals were admitted for manic-depressive disease. The youngest person admitted for manic-depressive illness was seventeen, although the admission record of "E. J.," first admitted in 1921 at age twenty-six, notes that she "has had several slight attacks in the last 12 years, since 13 years of age." All told, there were twelve individuals with a clear onset of illness under the age of twenty—this was 9 percent of all individuals admitted with manic depression.[45]

It is probably only a matter of time before this U.S. trend spreads to the rest of the world, leading to the admission of infants and young patients diagnosed with bipolar disorder to mental health facilities for treatment-induced mood disorders, psychoses, and other behavioral abnormalities. In the general medical wards, we can expect to see patients with diabetes, cardiovascular disturbances, and other physical problems that can be attributed to their diagnosis of bipolar disorder and their treatment with a cocktail of antipsychotic and anticonvulsant drugs beginning in early childhood. Will physicians and other practitioners be able to spot this problem and determine the appropriate course of action?

3

But Don't Call It Science

LAWRENCE DILLER

Most parents don't know him by name, but Joseph Biederman could be the most influential person in the United States when it comes to determining whether their children are mentally ill. Dr. Biederman has headed Harvard Medical School's Pediatric Psychopharmacology Unit for the past twenty years. In that capacity he has published (or at least coauthored) close to 2,000 articles on psychiatric drug use in children (often more than one hundred articles per year), primarily for the scientific community. Although he is not well known to the general public, Biederman commands huge power within the rather clubbish world of child psychiatry.

There are only about 6,000 child psychiatrists in all the United States. These professionals occupy the elite pinnacle of the mental health and treatment pyramid for children. At a professional presentation or in some obscure medical journal article, Dr. Biederman may merely mention the name of a new drug being used in his clinic for some childhood psychiatric condition, and within months several thousand children across the country will have been prescribed that drug. Such is the poor state of child psychiatric research, that rarely will these drugs have undergone the scrutiny that parents would expect before they are prescribed to their children. Clinical expertise and word of mouth are often all that doctors have to go on. And within that arcane world, Joseph Biederman's word is supreme.

A 1995 article on attention-deficit/hyperactivity disorder (ADHD) by Biederman and his colleagues announced that 23 percent of his clinic's ADHD pediatric population also met diagnostic criteria for bipolar disorder, representing a watershed change in America's view of children's mental health and illness.[1] Biederman had aroused controversy before. In 1996 he speculated that as many as 10 percent of America's children could benefit from stimulant medication for ADHD.[2] His influence and prescience were confirmed. A 2007 report on children's use of stimulant medication revealed that nationwide, slightly more than 10 percent of eleven-year-old insured white boys were taking stimulant medications such as Ritalin.[3]

Even so, this claim that nearly a quarter of ADHD patients were also bipolar initially met stunned astonishment and rejection from the general child psychiatric community.[4] Heretofore, bipolar disorder, once known as manic-depressive illness, was believed to be nearly nonexistent in the preteen population, and to be extremely rare even in teenagers.[5] But Biederman, continuing a trend begun in the 1980s, unilaterally expanded the boundaries of the condition by using a liberal semantic interpretation of the words set forth in the third edition of psychiatry's diagnostic bible, the *Diagnostic and Statistical Manual of Mental Orders (DSM-III)*.

A NEW ERA IN PSYCHIATRY:
FROM FREUD TO PSEUDOSCIENCE

The *DSM-III*, published in 1980, represented a revolutionary break from the sixty previous years in which Freudian theory had dominated the diagnosis and treatment of mental problems in America.[6] The *DSM-III* returned psychiatry to the medical model in which patients' behaviors were described rather than interpreted, and were collected in loosely defined groups of symptoms called "disorders." Although it was initially intended as an etiologically neutral document (with no causes ascribed to the disorders) to guide research in psychiatry, the *DSM-III* quickly assumed primacy as psychiatry's most important tool for diagnosing mental disorders that were now presumed to have a biological cause. But in order for the diagnoses listed in the *DSM-III* to have real medical value, the book would need to inform the clinician about the cause of the disease, the course of the disease, and the most effective method of treatment.[7] The majority of disorders listed in the *DSM-III* failed to meet these criteria because there was virtually no research upon which to base these groupings.[8] Rather they were based upon the opinions of clinicians anointed "experts" in their respective areas of expertise. Indeed, the popularity and success of the *DSM-III* may have had more to do with its convenience as a billing device for doctors and insurance companies than with any great leap in theoretical insight or practice. Nonetheless, the

DSM-III and its iterations (it is now in its fourth version, and a fifth edition is due in 2012) changed the psychiatric world of adults and children as we knew it.

DSM-III AND BIPOLAR DISORDER

Ironically, the best described and most cogent and practical entity included in the *DSM-III* was manic-depressive illness, which was officially renamed bipolar disorder (BD). The *DSM-III* provided a very specific definition of bipolar illness that included a regular cycle of alternating behavioral highs and lows. The highs could include quite outrageous behavior—delusional grandiosity and euphoria along with manic energy—a needed part of the diagnosis. The lows frequently involved severe depression and hopelessness culminating in thoughts and actions of self-mutilation or suicide. Substance abuse was (and continues to be) a regular accompanying condition to (or, in psychiatric jargon, "is comorbid with") bipolar illness.

Furthermore, the specificity of the bipolar disorder based upon previous research described in the *DSM-III* included only patients who were afflicted with a rather restricted similar set of symptoms and behaviors. Patterns of genetic inheritance were easily established (this does not negate the role of environment in the expression of this illness). There was also a very effective treatment for this more specific bipolar disorder. First discovered in Australia in the 1950s, lithium salts were found to be highly efficacious not only in treatment of the manic highs of bipolar disorder but also in the prevention of the destructive cycling.[9]

BIPOLAR DISORDER AND DIAGNOSTIC BRACKET CREEP

Beginning in the mid-1980s, criteria for bipolar disorder broadened. As a result, more and more adults were diagnosed with the condition. New diagnostic "refinements"—such as rapid cycling, bipolar types 1 and 2, and bipolar disorder without clear manic episodes—were unofficially added to the original diagnostic criteria listed in the *DSM-III* in order to encompass a new, more heterogeneous group of patients with a broader range of behavioral problems.

This "diagnostic bracket creep" beginning in the mid-1980s was not limited to the bipolar diagnosis but spread to many psychiatric diagnostic categories. Peter Kramer, in his best seller, *Listening to Prozac*, described the process by which the diagnosis of major depression in adults expanded to include less and less impaired individuals.[10] In hindsight, although many cultural and scientific factors were involved, the bottom line was the increasing commitment to the medical model by psychiatry to justify the growing use of psychiatric medications for treatment.

The times "they were a changing," but the introduction of Prozac in the late 1980s greatly speeded the process of transformation. The success of this drug and of the other SSRI antidepressants (selective serotonin reuptake inhibitors) that immediately followed it (especially Zoloft and Paxil) influenced the public perception that psychological disturbances were predominantly caused by faulty brain chemistry. "If a chemical improves someone's symptoms, they must be suffering from a chemical imbalance" became a central cultural tenet. Yet curiously, no one seemed to be promoting "aspirin deficiency" as a cause of headaches despite aspirin's effectiveness as a treatment.[11] Prozac's success also decreased the stigma of taking psychiatric medication for all psychiatric conditions.

According to the medical model, diagnosis should determine and direct treatment. But in a classic case of the horse following the cart, American psychiatry reversed the order of diagnosis directing treatment. The meaning of depression changed in order to justify prescribing these new drugs to an ever-increasing number of mildly unhappy or just overly sensitive people.

Although the practice of invoking a diagnosis to justify treatment occurs to an extent in all branches of medicine, it is most egregious in psychiatry. It is essential to note that there are no objective markers (blood tests, brain scans, or even psychometric gold standards) for any psychiatric disorder. In addition, the blatant disregard for the role of environmental factors such as family, job, school, neighborhood, and culture in the generation of a psychological disturbance makes psychiatric diagnoses the most vulnerable to this sort of scientific legerdemain.

A common—yet neither official nor approved—psychiatric diagnostic practice is the serial use of different drugs to confirm or negate a diagnosis, a process that has been facetiously called "diagnosis through pharmacological dissection." If a patient fails to respond to one or two first-line antidepressants, it is assumed that the diagnosis of depression is wrong and the patient must "have" something else. The number of patients with a bipolar diagnosis began to grow in the 1980s when first-line psychiatric drugs, such as the SSRI antidepressants and antianxiety agents, failed to control deviant behavior in adults. The shift to biological explanations and treatments already was so complete that physicians tended to overlook and discount environmental stressors and nondrug interventions such as lifestyle changes or psychotherapy.

Sedating medicines, approved for use by the FDA for such other indications as epilepsy or schizophrenia, were noted to be helpful in controlling the acting-out behaviors of adults. Anticonvulsant medications such as Dilantin and Tegretol and antipsychotic drugs such as Haldol or Mellaril found their way into the treatment armamentarium for bipolar disorder. With the growing popularity of the idea that mental illness is biologically based and should be treated with drugs, these medications became the next line of attack against virtually any kind of extreme problematic symptoms when the first-line drugs failed.

Drug companies were quick to take psychiatry's biological football and run with it. With every new medication licensed, the pharmaceutical industry sought and promoted "off-label" reasons (treatment for disorders not studied or FDA approved, but still legally prescribed) for using the drug. Industry-financed scientific studies and continuing medical education for doctors offered by industry-paid experts were thinly veiled advertisements to develop markets for these drugs. Along the way, the bipolar diagnosis became broader, more heterogeneous, and diluted, encompassing a wide and varied range of extreme adult behaviors.

In this process, lithium somehow lost its reputation as the mainstay drug for two reasons. First, because lithium was generic and cheap, there was no major financial incentive from drug companies to study or promote its use for this "new" bipolar disorder in adults. Second, because of the growing heterogeneity of this new bipolar disorder entity, the specificity of lithium treatment failed to help the much larger and far more diverse group of patients now included under the bipolar umbrella. Such industry-backed, nonspecific sedating, newer drugs as Risperdal, Zyprexa, Depakote, and Lamictal took the forefront of treatment. Lithium remained a choice, but only after these newer drugs failed to alter the course of the disorder. It was often then added to an existing cocktail of high-cost trade pharmaceuticals.

THE PEDIATRIC BIPOLAR DISORDER PHENOMENON

With this appreciation for the broad cultural and medical shifts in American psychiatry, we can now return to the pediatric bipolar phenomenon in America and Joseph Biederman's central role in it. The Harvard imprimatur gives the Biederman group extraordinary prestige, power, and legitimacy. In the mid-1990s, Biederman publicly stated in interviews that he couldn't understand why child psychiatry was lagging so far behind the adult world in its use of psychiatric drugs.[12] His clinic's commitment to psychopharmacology was total and groundbreaking. No doubt the children he was evaluating and treating had some of the most severe and recalcitrant problems—the kinds of cases that a tertiary referral medical center like the Massachusetts General Hospital attracts. Biederman's earlier research with ADHD children exemplified the best of what could come from the DSM model diagnosis.[13] The studies coming from the Pediatric Psychopharmacology clinic had a psychometric rigor, exactness, and breadth that were impressive and convincing (within the approved yet limited model of the *DSM-III*). His research won awards and acclaim internationally. But as we will see, the most fundamental aspects of any theoretical model are also the most subject to challenge.

THE LIMITS AND WEAKNESSES OF THE *DSM* FOR CHILDREN

The *DSM-III* was originally meant to serve as a theoretical and research model for problematic behavior. But very quickly the categories became reified to represent discrete biological entities, first adopted by doctors, and then taken up by the pharmaceutical industry and finally embraced by society at large. Without the research to support it, the *DSM-III* metamorphosed into a diagnostic system that claimed to have the rigor of the medical model. According to this model, a disorder is categorical—meaning that you either have it or you don't. But in the clinical real world, the symptoms associated with most children's psychiatric disorders are dimensional in nature, meaning that their intensity and frequency vary along a continuum.

In addition, few children's symptoms precisely match only one psychiatric disorder. Most children's problematic behaviors are a hodgepodge or combination of the specific categories of the *DSM*. For example, many children present with symptoms that combine symptoms typical of ADHD and oppositional defiant disorder. Psychiatry's official response to these ambiguities of real life is to label children with multiple, comorbid diagnoses or disorders, each "disease" often calling for another drug.

Furthermore, the *DSM* focuses on the symptoms and behavior of the *individual*, which may pragmatically "work" for adults, who are more independent. However, it is a far less useful construct for children, whose well-being is so dependent on their families, schools, and communities. The current *DSM* diagnoses only address the influence of genes and biology and barely acknowledge the role of environment at all.

Although anatomical or functional brain scans and family pedigrees can be brought forth and presented as "evidence" of a particular disorder, such reductionism misses the point that behavior is a function of the interaction between inherent factors *and* the environment. Indeed, there is very convincing neuroanatomical evidence from brain scans that demonstrate that experience directly changes the brain.[14] Genetic factors interplay with environment to create or prevent disease. For example, PKU deficiency is a genetically-based biochemical disorder of newborns that results in severe mental retardation unless a particular amino acid is eliminated from the diet. If foods with phenylalanine are removed, children with PKU deficiency develop entirely normally. Thus brain scans and family trees, which are regularly trumpeted as evidence of the biological and genetic nature of mental disorders, actually only indicate that nature and nurture interact in the development and prevention of these problems of living.

Yet when you try to engage the Harvard group in discussion about diagnosis, you encounter a rigidity of belief in the *DSM* that rivals the orthodox hegemony of the Freudian era in psychiatry.[15] This faith in the medical model of child psychiatry is more powerful and ominous than the previous ideology because it has the outer trappings of "science," and it is heavily supported by a powerful pharmaceutical industry. The drug industry has rewarded Biederman and his colleagues handsomely.[16] Biederman alone lists more then a dozen pharmaceutical companies that either fund his research or pay him directly as a consultant, speaker, author, or researcher.[17]

Much has been written in recent years about the inevitable conflict of interest when drug companies fund medical researchers.[18] Yet virtually all doctors who are richly compensated by the pharmaceutical industry decry and deny any influence, although more dispassionate surveys indicate otherwise.[19] Even presuming that the Harvard group has remained above the influence of the pharmaceutical industry's generous support of their research, there is no question that drug company money has allowed Biederman and his colleagues an enormous supported platform from which to express their ideas to other doctors and the public.[20]

In the ongoing debate of nature versus nurture, reasonable arguments become derailed over selective examples. Surely, at the extremes of certain behavioral problems, there are rather pure examples of children with one disorder or another in which neurological factors predominate to support a biologically based *DSM* diagnosis. An example could be the extreme hyperactivity of ADHD that sometimes presents with mental retardation. On the other side of the debate, some extremists propose that bipolar disorder and ADHD "do not exist" but are solely social constructions created to control children's behavior with drugs.[21] But proponents of the extreme biological, or "nature," position are equally guilty of ignoring the environmental contribution to problem behavior. Here the slippery semantic slope of the language of the *DSM* allows for fairly normal children or children going through a normative crisis or phase of emotional development (e.g., adolescence) to be diagnosed, labeled, categorized, and treated like children with very severe behavioral or emotional problems with a large neurological component.

To a degree, the side of the debate one supports, reflects one's patient population. The Massachusetts General/Harvard group tends to see children with very extreme behavior with a higher-than-average neurological contribution, whose families have previously pursued psychotherapy and medication to no avail before entering the holy temple of the tertiary medical center. Therefore, the search was on by the mid-1990s for a diagnosis that could capture this group of very disturbed children, whose symptoms were not tractable on the standard stimulants or antidepressants.

The introduction of a pediatric version of bipolar disorder (akin to juvenile versus adult-onset diabetes) seemed to fit the bill. The proposed pediatric version of bipolar disorder was said to be more severe than its adult counterpart. It featured an unrelenting "rapid cycling" more consistent with the most serious treatment-resistant versions of the adult disorder.[22] Yet this "new" pediatric rendition of the problem retained the name of the adult diagnosis, while significantly altering the criteria. In the process both the professional and lay audiences continue to be confused about whether the pediatric version carries with it the same lifelong implication of the adult disorder. In truth, no one knows the answer because there are no data.[23] It seems that pediatric bipolar advocates want it both ways. They want criteria different from the already broad and ambiguous adult version of bipolar disorder, but the same name, the same grave long-term prognosis for these children, and the same biological interventions used with bipolar adults.

Biederman's claim in 1995 that 23 percent of his clinic's ADHD pediatric population also had bipolar disorder was initially met with shock and some derision from the rest of the child psychiatric community. "ADHD is for irritable and irritating kids. Bipolar disorder is for *very* irritable and *very* irritating kids," one psychiatrist cynically remarked. Indeed, the focus of Biederman's pediatric bipolar symptomatology was on acting out, throwing temper tantrums, and displaying violent behavior—previously associated with extreme oppositional defiant disorder (ODD) or conduct disorder (CD). It is noteworthy that both ODD and CD are believed to be strongly influenced by environmental factors (even within the *DSM* model, e.g., oppositional to whom or what?). Even more important, many older studies had demonstrated the failure of psychiatric medication to make a big difference in children with either of these two conditions. Therefore, if the Harvard clinic, as a place of last resort, was to help this group of very disabled, acting-out children, some diagnostic cover had to be conceived to justify the use of the next level of psychoactive drug interventions (after stimulants and antidepressants had failed to control the behavior). Eureka! Expand the bipolar diagnosis!

Besides the general skepticism, more specific criticisms were directed at the Harvard group's claims about pediatric bipolar illness by the only other medical center conducting research on pediatric bipolar disorder at that time: the St. Louis group at Washington University headed by Barbara Geller.[24] Geller's criteria were and continue to be more restrictive and selective for the early-onset bipolar diagnosis. Children have to demonstrate euphoria, grandiosity, lack of sleep, hypersexuality, and other symptoms that are associated with the classic definition of mania. If those types of symptomatic behaviors are required, the number of kids meeting bipolar criteria decreases dramatically.

Even so, defining manic behavior in a child or teen is a slippery slope. Aren't children entitled to fantasize? What seven-year-old boy hasn't imagined that he is a superhero, be it Superman or Spiderman? Where is the line between delusion and fantasy in a younger child? And what about the energy, intensity, moodiness, grandiosity, and despair of teenagers? From the time of Shakespeare's *Romeo and Juliet* (and going back even further to the Greeks), to more recent twentieth-century versions of teen angst, adolescence has been considered a phase when crises and extremes are normative.

Bipolar diagnosis proponents defend their criteria with case histories marked by extremes of behavior that are dangerous, unsettling, and very out of control. But these proponents fail to acknowledge and sufficiently address how these criteria are employed in the general community. The most egregious example of this kind of blinkered thinking can be found in psychiatrist Demetri Papolos's best-selling book, *The Bipolar Child: The Definitive and Reassuring Guide to Childhood's Most Misunderstood Disorder* (coauthored with his wife Janice Papolos).[25] "Once you see what this looks like, you can't mistake it," Papolos said in a published interview.[26] He also claimed that he couldn't recall a child referred to him over the past seven years who didn't have bipolar disorder.

Papolos comes across as a successful but dangerous clinical farce. He has had tremendous influence on a desperate group of parents who are seeking solutions to their children's problems. Papolos's answer is easy and seductive—pediatric bipolar disorder is a common childhood illness that has been misunderstood and underdiagnosed

until now. He bases his practice on the research of Biederman and Geller.

Organized psychiatry's continued call for better diagnosis in the community is ineffectual and hypocritical. Although Papolos may be one of the worst abusers of the bipolar diagnosis in children, doctors' entrenched practices do not tend to change as a result of the guidelines of professional organizations. Only economic factors, the threat of legal action, or very negative publicity (e.g., children's deaths while taking antidepressants) have widespread influence on doctors' pre-scribing practices and treatment. Furthermore, better diagnosis has come to mean being seen by a board-certified child psychiatrist. But the reality is, if you take your son or daughter to a child psychiatrist, the likelihood of not receiving one or more psychiatric medication pre-scriptions is only one in ten.[27]

STORIES FROM THE "BIPOLAR" SPECTRUM

I begin my clinical tales with an individual who would meet my criteria for what we are calling bipolar disorder today. The names and some of the details of the individuals and families have been changed. I met Joe, the father of a particular child I evaluated in the early 1980s before the bipolar label was broadened and diluted. Joe had been diag-nosed with manic depression and had taken (but was not currently taking) lithium when I met him for the first time. I was impressed by his energy, and by his intensity and rigidity in following ideas about his business that I considered very unlikely to succeed—ideas that were outlandish, even bordering on the delusional. He had similarly rigid ideas about parenting that led to multiple clashes with his wife and children.

Not surprisingly his superhuman efforts (eighty-hour work-weeks) to make his business succeed against all odds culminated in business and personal disaster. He fell into a deep depression, talked of suicide, looked disheveled, and ultimately was hospitalized. Even-tually he recovered and began taking lithium again. I subsequently met him again after he had resumed taking his medication. He struck me as subdued but more reasonable compared to his previously unmedicated state. He also had a noticeable fine tremor on the drug, which he accepted as a condition of maintaining his mental balance.

Relentless pursuit of an unrealistic goal in spite of its almost inevitable failure is a salient feature of real manic depression. We can all relate to trying hard and then failing. I strive with passion and energy to shift professional and public thinking about children, psy-chiatric diagnosis, and drugs. It takes extra time from my life, especially from my evenings and weekends. I get paid for very little of the work I do in this arena. But I don't stay awake for ninety-six consecutive hours thinking, planning, and working on my passion. I don't believe I am on speaking terms with President Bush, or even with Oprah. I have dinner every evening with my family and still find time to play tennis two or three times a week. I don't think I'm bipolar or even hypomanic. You may not agree.

Doctors describe hypomania as a potentially very productive, and even beneficial state, maintained successfully for a period of time by many people working in industry or for themselves. However, we all need a break or a rest. Those who don't find a balance may also find themselves sinking into a depressive state, even if it doesn't include suicidal thinking. This continuum between mental health and illness is by no means exclusive to bipolar disorder. Children break down every day in my office but no more than a dozen or so of the 2,500 I've seen have met my criteria for a major mental disorder.

Two "bipolar" children I have seen professionally provide insight into the reality of frontline clinical practice. In actuality, scores of children have been referred to my practice either with the bipolar label or to be considered for the diagnosis. I've chosen to briefly describe my experiences with Steven, who was seven when I first met him, and Gloria, who was fourteen. Steven represents an example of the abuse of the bipolar diagnosis. Gloria, however, could be the rare example of an adolescent who may actually prove over time to have bipolar disorder as an adult. The children's names and other identifying family data have been changed for confidentiality.

Jody, Steven's mother, complained that Steven "exploded" over small changes in his routine, becoming physically violent and uncontrollable. His behavior included kicking doors, hitting himself, throwing things, pulling items off shelves, and trying to hit or bite his mother. He would talk about "killing," "wishing I were dead," and mentioning something about a "fork in my head." His father Eugene's interactions with Steven weren't as intense, but he acknowledged that when the family (which included a younger sister and brother) was all together, he also had difficulty containing Steven's anger at times. Steven would also lose control in front of his grandparents, who were frequent caregivers for the children, but he never displayed this behavior with anyone outside the family or at school.

Steven's mother also noted that he was an anxious child who worried about school and would wake up in the middle of the night frightened to be by himself. He had been seen six months earlier by a therapist who believed he had Asperger's syndrome, a relational disorder considered to be a mild, high-functioning form of autism. In the past, children who would have been considered shy or socially awkward now frequently carry the Asperger's label. Eight sessions of psychotherapy primarily directed to Steven failed to improve his symptoms.

His mother then took Steven to a respected behavioral–psychiatric group (three months before I met him). The child psychiatrist in the group diagnosed Steven with bipolar disorder and first prescribed Neurontin (an anticonvulsant that was successfully promoted for off-label use for bipolar disorder until 2005 when reports of its side effects and illegal advertising led to its decline). This drug allegedly caused Steven to have insomnia and five days of rage. Risperdal was substituted, and Depakote (another anticonvulsant) was added. Steven's appetite increased significantly after starting the Risperdal (prodigious weight gain can be a side effect).

Steven's parents were referred to me by his pediatrician, who was concerned about the use of these medications in a seven-year-old and because the behavior problems continued unabated. I first met Steven with his entire family (including the grandparents). I was struck by his unease in greeting me and in participating in conversation (especially when compared to his younger siblings, who seemed more easygoing). His two-year-old brother dominated the meeting with demands and limit testing of both parents. Steven was relatively self-controlled.

Meeting Steven alone one time confirmed my feelings that he was a fairly anxious child who regularly tested his parents' limit setting with displays of out-of-control behavior. He was unhappy and confused about his own behavior. He said he was a bad boy and that something was wrong with his brain. He also confirmed what I had noticed in the family visit—that there was serious disagreement and tension between the parents.

Indeed, in a separate meeting with the parents, it became clear that their marriage of twelve years was on the rocks. Jody's anxieties about herself and her children also were quite noticeable. Her profound sense of inadequacy and worry about her children greatly compromised her ability to set limits for them, and tended to reinforce Steven's own worries about himself and his inability to control his fears and anger when he wasn't rescued or didn't get what he wanted.

I worked primarily with the parents (especially Jody) and the school over the next year or so in weekly or every-other-weekly sessions. Eventually Jody was somewhat more successful in setting limits for her children, although getting Steven to school became increasingly difficult. He was home schooled with a public school teacher for about four months. I worked to discontinue the Depakote successfully, but the family continued to employ the Risperdal, especially at night to attenuate Steven's fears and anger. Meanwhile the marriage continued to deteriorate with outward displays of marital tension and arguing in front of the children.

After a year Eugene left the home and moved in with his mother. Steven's behavior deteriorated at Jody's house, and with my assent the parents agreed that Steven should live primarily with his father. Steven's symptoms and behavior markedly improved under his father's primary custodial care. He started attending regular school almost immediately upon living with his father. He continued to have temper tantrums when he was with his mother, particularly when he spent the night at her house. Ultimately, Jody moved out of state for financial reasons, taking the two younger children and agreeing with Eugene that Steven should remain with him.

Over a three-month period, his father and I weaned Steven off the Risperdal (which was still being used at night) so that eighteen months after I first met him Steven was no longer on psychiatric medication, was doing reasonably well in a normal school environment, and was living with his father. I believe Steven's rather remarkable recovery reflected Eugene's better ability at setting limits and remaining less anxious when Steven became upset. The decrease in overt marital conflict after the separation no doubt also eased tensions, not only for Steven but also for his sister and brother.

When I met Gloria for the first time, she was a perky fourteen-year-old girl with a wild sense of humor. She'd been "diagnosed bipolar" four years earlier and had been in individual therapy because she had been cutting herself six months before that. Her psychiatrist had prescribed Topomax (one of the newer anticonvulsants), Seroquel (an antipsychotic), Effexor XR (ostensibly for depression), and lithium. She complained frequently of being tired during the day. The family had turned to me because they were unhappy with her psychiatrist, who increased her dosage or added another drug to her regimen every time they complained about Gloria's behavior or her lack of progress. Neither Gloria nor her parents felt connected to the psychiatrist. They found me through their managed care insurance plan.

I felt that Gloria was an intelligent but depressed adolescent. She was very unhappy with herself, regarding herself as a mental case and a failure. She was also very unhappy with her parents, who always fought. Tina, her overwhelmed mother, tried to maintain some order and rules in the household for Gloria and her older brother and sister. The two older siblings had been relatively successful in school and were fairly independent. Gloria, however, seemed more needy and tested her parents' rules continuously.

Ralph, Gloria's father, was himself a depressed man, angry with his wife for openly maintaining an affair with another man for the past five years. He wanted her to end the relationship, but she refused. He repeatedly threatened to kill himself if she left him for the other man. The affair and the father's threats were open knowledge in the family. Ralph also appeared to have a not-so-secret alliance with Gloria to subvert Tina's rules (incest was denied by all parties involved).

Gloria struck me as a potentially *forme fruste* adult bipolar patient. She had bursts of enthusiasm and energy for goals that at times seemed unrealistic. She would then lapse, like many teenagers, in terms of responsibility (e.g., in getting a certain school project done in time), and then want to give up entirely in school. Some of her ideas about relationships with her peers were out of proportion to their real intensity and meaning. Her highs and lows were just a bit beyond what many struggling teenagers experience.

I believed that Gloria's parents did not know how to set and enforce consistent standards for their children, but for the two older siblings, consistency and follow-through were not as critical. By contrast, Gloria's intensity and persistence made firm, consistent parenting more important. However, her parents' ambivalence about setting limits and their preoccupation with their marital problems precluded their providing Gloria with the necessary structure and rules she needed to succeed. Their weaknesses as parents allowed Gloria to avoid learning to cope with frustration. Gloria pushed and pushed until she got what she wanted or was rescued. But as she grew older, these strategies began failing her in the outside world and with peers.

I agreed to be responsible for Gloria's medication only if I had the cooperation and participation of both parents in the treatment. They both agreed, and I began to see Gloria and her family, alternating between seeing Gloria with her family or parents one week and seeing Gloria alone the next. At certain times I also met with the parents alone and individually. Working with the parents wasn't easy but I managed to convince Ralph to support some of Tina's rules. Gloria's school grades went from Fs to Bs over the course of the year.

I was able to discontinue Gloria's Topomax without any relapse, but she continued on the other three medications. The marriage remained highly problematic and upsetting for all of the children. I worked with Ralph to help him manage his feelings toward Tina and cope with a potential separation. He was able to tell me that he would not kill himself; however, I could tell he was unhappy with the direction in which treatment for the family was proceeding. He failed to bring Gloria to my office on several occasions when it was his turn (the parents alternated in this responsibility). After fifteen months and several warnings, I terminated my relationship with the family because of parental noncooperation. I was able to find another doctor for Gloria to monitor her medication.

Twenty months later Tina called me and asked if I would be Gloria's doctor (meaning, would I prescribe medication?) again. She told me that Ralph had voluntarily left the household three months earlier and that Gloria was doing well in school but was still taking medication. I agreed to meet Gloria and Tina. Gloria at age seventeen appeared quite mature and healthy. Her attitude toward starting her junior year in high school was positive, and her mother made a commitment to attend sessions when I deemed her presence necessary.

Gloria was only taking lithium and Effexor on this second go-round. She felt that both were helpful, although I wasn't certain how regularly she was taking either. A lithium level revealed blood serum levels in the low but therapeutic range. Gloria had embarked on an ambitious health-related curriculum at her high school, but within three weeks she had transferred out of the more difficult classes. By the end of the first quarter, her school performance was just mediocre, and she was disappointed in herself. However, she met regularly with an individual therapist and was not especially depressed or unhappy.

Gloria may still be struggling with her personality into her twenties, and she may suffer from bipolar disorder in adulthood. But she also might make it as an entertainer. She had an intelligent mordant wit—and she could imitate many adults and teens she knew to perfection. She had the air of reckless self-deprecation seen in many stand-up comedians. "Aren't those comedians bipolar?" would be an expected challenge. They may be bipolar, but successful comedians couldn't rise to fame while taking Risperdal.

I have described two children who were diagnosed as bipolar and taking multiple medications, whose parents eventually separated. Proponents of the bipolar diagnosis could say simply that these children were incorrectly diagnosed as bipolar. Yet in the real world of community psychiatry, extenuating circumstances within the family are often ignored in determining a diagnosis. The child is treated with drugs to either attenuate or control the problem behaviors, which may also be self-injurious.

Both these children were desperately unhappy and their parents were overwhelmed. One needn't invoke sinister motives on the part of parents and doctors in having these children medicated. Both families had first sought counseling services. As is typical, both therapies were directed to the children and barely included the parents or family. When the therapy proved inadequate, both the families and their therapists understandably wondered whether the problems were caused by chemical imbalances that should be treated with drugs. The intensity and frequency of the children's symptoms, the ineffectiveness of less potent first-line psychiatric drugs such as antidepressants and stimulants, and the opinions and attitudes of the families and professional caregivers determined whether they met bipolar criteria.

I do not blame parents when I acknowledge their role in children's symptomatology and their responsibility as agents of change. Most of the children labeled bipolar *are* "very irritable and irritating." They are not easy kids to raise. They require a degree of consistency and confidence that may be beyond the skill level of most parents in a normal family setting. Poor marriages can lead to troubled kids, but certainly difficult kids, who stay that way despite their parents' efforts, can also lead to worsening marriages.

However, neither do I entirely exonerate parents or chaotic family situations as contributors to their children's behavior. Troubled marriages, divorce, and chaos seem more the rule than the exception for the families of children who are being considered candidates for the bipolar diagnosis. In the world of *DSM* diagnosis, these factors are not considered or viewed only as "proof" of a genetic or biological predisposition to mental problems in the children.

I am not even against medicating some of these children with these sedating drugs. After I've worked with a family for several months and recognize that a young child's choice may come down to foster care because of the child's out-of-control behavior or the risk of physical abuse in his own home, I might prescribe low-dose Risperdal—in part because I know that if the child goes to a foster home he is likely to receive two or three medications. Under my care he will take only one.

But I'm still very unlikely to label this child as bipolar. I frankly don't know what bipolar illness looks like in a preteen. I won't accept either the criteria of Biederman or Geller until there have been some real prospective studies following these kids into their mid-twenties. By then most children are finished with their adolescent testing and find their way out of school into jobs and relationships. If these young adults are still acting outrageously with manic ups and suicidal downs, I could be prepared to call them bipolar and offer them medication. Lithium is a difficult drug to take, but it was a lifesaver for countless persons with manic depression before the dilution of the bipolar diagnosis.

PRESCHOOL BIPOLAR DISORDER—THE LINE IS CROSSED

I'm not sure what to think when I read of a study by the Biederman camp on the use of Risperdal in preschoolers diagnosed with bipolar disorder.[28] I can actually imagine a need to understand the dosages and side effects when using antipsychotics in children this young. Like it or not, as any sociologist or anthropologist will tell you when observing America's child-rearing practices today, if children don't learn compliance (obeying others) interactionally with their parents and teachers, compliance will be achieved chemically. So some children this young will be treated with sedating drugs to manage their behavior.

Even the American Academy of Child and Adolescent Psychiatry (AACAP) in its guidelines for the assessment and treatment of pediatric bipolar disorder is clear about the controversy over the diagnosis, especially in young children. "The debate and controversy over juvenile bipolar disorder are not whether there are a significant number of youths who are explosive, dysregulated, and emotionally labile. ... These difficulties and concerns are commonplace. ... The debate is whether these problems in youths are best characterized as bipolar disorder and, more important[ly], whether juvenile mania is the same illness as that classically described in adults."[29]

The AACAP goes further in its official recommendations about applying the bipolar label and the consequent pharmacological treatment for preschoolers. Recommendation 5 in bold and capital letters states: "THE DIAGNOSTIC VALIDITY OF BIPOLAR DISORDER IN YOUNG CHILDREN HAS YET TO BE ESTABLISHED. CAUTION MUST BE TAKEN BEFORE APPLYING THIS DIAGNOSIS IN PRESCHOOL CHILDREN."[30]

THE DEATH OF REBECCA RILEY AND MORAL RESPONSIBILITY

I am not as restrained in my uncertainty. The public was shockingly introduced to the bipolar diagnosis in preschoolers when the media reported on the death of Rebecca Riley, a four-year-old from the Boston area.[31] The circumstances surrounding this child's death are unclear. The courts will decide whether her parents were guilty of intentionally overdosing her with clonidine (one of three psychiatric drugs she was prescribed) or whether her death was accidental. But we do know that a respected Tufts University–affiliated child psychiatrist had "diagnosed" Rebecca with bipolar disorder at age two and was treating her at the time of her death.

I resent and am astounded by the pseudoscience that labels children as young as two with the lifelong sentence of this condition. Rebecca's family life, at least as reported in the media, seemed highly dysfunctional, yet Rebecca was the one assigned this diagnosis and treated with multiple drugs.[32] It may be no accident that the Tufts

Medical Center is only a bit down the road from Massachusetts General Hospital.

The Tufts psychiatrist, like the showman Papolos, could not have invoked the bipolar diagnosis without the "science" coming from Joseph Biederman's clinic. For this reason, if he does not speak out quickly and forcefully about the misuse of this label and about the mass drugging of acting-out children in our country, then he bears a moral responsibility for this current tragedy and for any future catastrophes, not to mention responsibility for the wholesale sedation of children for what is really a crisis in public health. The silence of organized psychiatry around this issue is also deafening. Perhaps by the time these labeled kids reach their twenties, the bipolar diagnosis will become almost as meaningless as ADHD is now (The term today refers more to a lifestyle or personality type rather than to a mental illness.) I haven't even mentioned the legal and actuarial implications of this diagnosis (e.g., the employment implications, insurance restrictions, etc.) once these kids reach majority age and are on their own. I simply don't believe that science leads us to label two- and three-year-olds with the bipolar diagnosis. If this is science, then it may be similar to the "science" that once justified ice-pick lobotomies and insulin coma shock treatments, and blamed mothers for their children's autism. The doctors who subscribed to such "science" believed their experiments and research were for the good of the individual and the community, and based their treatments on the assumptions of their day. Only with time, I suppose, will we know how history judges the psychiatric research and medical practice on children that is taking place in Boston these days. Until then I remain very, very concerned.

4

Creating the Bipolar Child: How Our Drug-Based Paradigm of Care Is Fueling an Epidemic of Disabling Mental Illness in Children

ROBERT WHITAKER

There has been an astonishing rise in the diagnosis of juvenile bipolar disorder in the past fifteen years, so much so that a disorder that was once seen as rare in children and teenagers is now said to affect 1 percent—or even 2 percent—of all youth. There are two prevailing perspectives about this rise. First, there are those who say that this is a disorder that previously went unrecognized, and thus the rise simply reflects a new awareness about bipolar illness in children. Second, there are those who argue that the rise is due to greatly expanded boundaries for diagnosing the disorder so that it is principally a labeling issue, yet another example of psychiatry's pathologizing of childhood. However, there is a third perspective to consider, and it is this: children and adolescents initially diagnosed with ADHD and depression are being treated with medications that can trigger symptoms said to characterize juvenile bipolar disorder, and many who suffer such drug-induced symptoms are then diagnosed with this more serious psychiatric "illness." Moreover, once children are diagnosed with bipolar disorder, they are routinely treated with a powerful drug cocktail that puts them on a path toward lifelong disability. Our drug-based paradigm of care is turning many children with behavioral and emotional problems, often mild in kind, into lifelong psychiatric patients.

A HISTORY OF PSYCHIATRIC DRUG USE

In order to appreciate how our drug-based paradigm of care may be fueling an epidemic of bipolar disorder in children, it is necessary to take a big-picture look at what science has revealed about this paradigm of care over the past fifty years. That history reveals why psychiatric drugs are bound to be problematic for many patients over the long term and why they may act as disease-inducing agents.

The modern era of psychopharmacology is said to date to 1955, when chlorpromazine, marketed as Thorazine, was introduced in mental hospitals. Thorazine is remembered today as the first antipsychotic drug. After it came on the market, pharmaceutical companies quickly began introducing other disorder-specific drugs—most notably antidepressants and antianxiety medications. These drugs correct "chemical imbalances" in the brain, or so the public is told. However, a review of the scientific literature reveals that the precise opposite is true: people diagnosed with mental disorders do not have any known chemical imbalance, and the drugs prescribed for these disorders all work by perturbing—sometimes profoundly—neurotransmitter systems in the brain. These medications actually create "chemical imbalances" in the brain, and once this is understood, it is easy to see why their long-term widespread use has correlated with an astonishing rise in the number of disabled mentally ill adults in the United States over the past fifty years.

The Chemical Imbalance Hypothesis of Schizophrenia

The chemical imbalance theory of mental disorders got its start in 1963, when Swedish pharmacologist Arvid Carlsson determined that chlorpromazine and other antipsychotic medications powerfully inhibited the activity of the neurotransmitter dopamine in the brain. However, it was clear early on that these drugs were causing a pathological deficiency in dopamine transmission: patients treated with chlorpromazine and other antipsychotics regularly developed Parkinsonian symptoms, a disease that results from the loss of dopaminergic neurons in the basal ganglia, the area of the brain that controls motor movement. Parkinsonian symptoms appear when dopamine levels drop to about 20 percent of normal, and so the drugs, by blocking dopamine, were evidently causing a similar deficiency. Yet Carlsson and others speculated that because antipsychotics had an apparent therapeutic effect and alleviate the symptoms of psychosis, perhaps schizophrenia was caused by too much dopamine activity. Moreover, it was known that amphetamines, which release dopamine, can cause psychosis—another bit of evidence that schizophrenia might be caused by too much dopamine. Carlsson's hypothesis was in every way a reasonable one.

There were two possible ways that a dopaminergic system could be overactive. Neurotransmitters work in this manner: A "presynaptic" neuron releases the neurotransmitter into the synaptic cleft (the space between neurons), and then the neurotransmitter binds with receptors on a "postsynaptic" neuron. Carlsson's dopamine hypothesis suggested that either the presynaptic neurons were releasing too much of the neurotransmitter or else the postsynaptic neurons had too many receptors and thus were "hypersensitive" to dopamine.

To explore the first possibility, investigators measured levels of dopamine metabolites (or breakdown products) in their patients' blood, urine, and cerebrospinal fluid, because this provided an indirect gauge of dopamine release in the brain. One of the first such studies was done in 1974 by Malcolm Bowers at Yale. He determined that levels of dopamine metabolites in unmedicated schizophrenics were normal. "Our findings," he wrote, "do not furnish neurochemical evidence for an overarousal in these patients emanating from a midbrain dopamine system."[1]

Others soon reported similar findings. In 1975 Robert Post at the National Institute of Mental Health found no evidence of elevated dopamine levels in twenty nonmedicated schizophrenia patients compared to healthy controls.[2] Three different research teams determined in autopsy studies that drug-free schizophrenics apparently had normal dopamine levels. All of this led John Haracz, a neuroscientist at the University of California, Los Angeles, to conclude in 1982: "Direct support [for the dopamine hypothesis] is either uncompelling or has not been widely replicated."[3]

Having failed to find that unmedicated schizophrenics have abnormally high levels of dopamine, researchers turned their attention to whether their postsynaptic neurons had too many dopamine receptors. At first blush researchers found just that. In 1978 Tyrone Lee and Philip Seeman at the University of Toronto reported in *Nature* that at autopsy the brains of schizophrenics had 50 percent or more dopamine receptors than healthy controls.[4] But the patients studied had been on neuroleptics and, as Lee and Seeman readily acknowledged, it was possible that the neuroleptics had caused the abnormality. Animal studies and other postmortem studies soon revealed that was indeed the case. Investigators in the United States, England, and Germany all determined that taking neuroleptics led to an increase in brain dopamine receptors, and they found little evidence of higher-than-normal receptor levels prior to drug use.[5] "From our data," German investigators wrote in 1989, "we conclude that changes in [receptor density] values in schizophrenics are entirely iatrogenic [drug caused]." [6]

Thus, after more than two decades of research, investigators came to a sobering conclusion. They had speculated that schizophrenics naturally suffered from overactive dopamine systems but had found that this wasn't so. As John Kane wrote in 1994: "A simple dopaminergic excess model of schizophrenia is no longer credible."[7] But even more worrisome, they had discovered that the brain responds to a neuroleptic as though it were a pathological insult.

At a therapeutic dose, chlorpromazine and other standard antipsychotics may occupy 70 to 90 percent of all D_2 receptors (a particular type of dopamine receptor). In response to the blockade, the brain tries to compensate in two ways. First, for at least a short period of time, presynaptic dopaminergic neurons apparently go into hypergear, pumping out more dopamine than normal. Then the brain cells, as if they are burning out, gradually slow down to the point that they are releasing less dopamine than normal. Some dopaminergic cells turn quiescent, and others begin firing in irregular patterns.[8] Second, as the research by Seeman and Lee first revealed, the brain sprouts more dopamine receptors. In short, the drug treatment causes the very abnormality hypothesized to cause schizophrenia in the first place.

Thus, the findings from thirty years of research on the dopamine hypothesis of schizophrenia work can be summarized as follows:

1. Studies failed to find that people so diagnosed had overactive dopamine systems.
2. The drugs work by blocking 70 to 90 percent of D_2 receptors in the brain.
3. In response, the brain tries to compensate by pumping out more dopamine for a short period of time and by increasing the density of its dopamine receptors.

The Chemical Imbalance Theory of Depression

The story of the chemical imbalance theory of depression is similar in kind. Once researchers in the 1960s came to understand that tricyclics, which had become the antidepressants of choice, affected both norepinephrine and serotonin, it was hypothesized that depressed people had abnormal levels of these brain chemicals. When Eli Lilly introduced Prozac (fluoxetine) in 1988, this hypothesis was refined. Because fluoxetine blocked the normal reuptake of serotonin, and thus theoretically raised levels of the neurotransmitter in the synaptic cleft, psychiatric researchers reasoned that depressed people had abnormally low levels of serotonin.

Researchers investigating the serotonin hypothesis of depression utilized many of the same methods that had been employed to investigate the dopamine hypothesis of schizophrenia, and the line of research came to the same dead end. "I spent the first several years of my career doing full-time research on brain serotonin metabolism, but I never saw any convincing evidence that any psychiatric disorder, including depression, results from a deficiency of brain serotonin," said Stanford psychiatrist David Burns.[9] In his 1998 book *Blaming the Brain,* neuroscientist Elliot Valenstein reviewed the history of research into the serotonin hypothesis of depression and concluded: "Although it is often stated with great confidence that depressed people have a serotonin or norepinephrine deficiency, the evidence actually contradicts these claims."[10] More recently, David Healy, an English psychiatrist who has written extensively on the history of psychiatry, said the serotonin hypothesis of depression should be brushed into the dustbin, where other such discredited psychiatric theories can be found: "The serotonin theory of depression is comparable to the masturbatory theory of insanity."[11]

However, Prozac and other selected serotonin reuptake inhibitor (SSRI) antidepressants do *perturb* serotonin function, and once again researchers discovered that the brain goes through a series of compensatory adaptations. Because an SSRI blocks the normal reuptake of serotonin, the brain responds by toning down its whole serotonergic system. Neurons both release less serotonin and down-regulate (or decrease) their number of serotonin receptors. These drugs, concluded Princeton neuroscientist Barry Jacobs, "alter the level of synaptic transmission beyond the physiologic range under [normal] environmental/biological conditions. Thus, any behavioral or physiologic change produced under these conditions might more appropriately be considered pathologic, rather than reflective of the normal biological role of serotonin."[12]

A PARADIGM FOR UNDERSTANDING
ALL PSYCHIATRIC DRUGS

Drug companies and psychiatrists have used the chemical imbalance metaphor to explain other mental disorders as well. For example, Ritalin and other stimulants used to treat ADHD release dopamine, so investigators theorized that ADHD was caused by abnormally low levels of dopamine. But once again, no such deficiency was ever found in children so diagnosed. Although pharmaceutical companies may still be peddling the paradigm, most researchers today admit that the entire chemical imbalance theory of mental disorders never panned out. "We have hunted for big simple neurochemical explanations for psychiatric disorders and we have not found them," confessed psychiatrist Kenneth Kendler, coeditor-in-chief of *Psychological Medicine* in 2005.[13]

In 1996 neuroscientist Steven Hyman, then head of the National Institute of Mental Health, took stock of what decades of research had shown and set forth a paradigm for understanding how all psychiatric drugs work. Antipsychotics, antidepressants, and antianxiety drugs, he wrote, all "create perturbations in neurotransmitter functions."[14] In response, he noted, the brain goes through a series of compensatory adaptations. If a drug blocks dopamine activity, the brain tries to become more sensitive to this chemical. If a drug blocks the reuptake of serotonin, the brain tones down its serotonergic system. As part of this adaptation process, Hyman noted, there are also changes in intracellular signaling pathways and gene expression. After a few weeks, Hyman concluded, the patient's brain is functioning in a manner that is "qualitatively as well as quantitatively different from the normal state."[15]

Thus, science provides this big-picture view of psychiatric disorders and the drugs used to treat those conditions: people diagnosed with mental disorders have no known chemical imbalance in the brain. The drugs work by perturbing neurotransmitter activity in the brain to a degree that could be considered pathological. To compensate, the brain goes through a series of adaptations that leaves it functioning in an *abnormal* manner.

THE ASTONISHING RISE IN THE NUMBER OF DISABLED MENTALLY ILL ADULTS

Once psychiatric drugs are understood to be chemical imbalancers, it is easy to understand why their use might prove to be so problematic over the long term. Although the drugs might ameliorate a target symptom over the short term, one would expect these agents to trigger a host of adverse events, both physical and mental, over longer periods of time. As E. Fuller Torrey observed in *The Invisible Plague,* conditions that "disrupt brain chemistry may cause delusions, hallucinations, disordered thinking, and mood swings—the symptoms of insanity."[16] He noted that infectious agents, tumors, metabolic and toxic disorders, and various diseases can all affect the brain in this manner. Because psychiatric drugs also disrupt brain chemistry, one would expect that they would also frequently stir the "symptoms of insanity."

The fact that the drugs may act as disease-causing agents—in the population at large and over long periods of time—can be seen in the astonishing rise in the number of disabled mentally ill persons in the United States since the 1950s, when the first generation of psychiatric drugs was introduced into the market. This rise can be tracked in two ways.

Table 4.1 Patient Care Episodes

Year	Total No. of Episodes	Episodes per 100,000 Population*
1955	1,675,352	1,028
1965	2,636,525	1,376
1969	3,682,454	1,853
1971	4,190,913	2,026
1975	6,857,597	3,182
1983	7,194,038	3,084
1986	7,885,618	3,295
1990	8,620,628	3,491
1992	8,824,701	3,580
1994	9,584,216	3,680
1998	10,549,951	3,903
2000	10,741,243	3,806

Source: Data from the U.S. Department of Health and Human Services, Substance Abuse and Mental Health Services Administration (2002). *Mental Health, United States, 2002.*
*Calculated by the U.S. Bureau of the Census.

First, the U.S. Department of Health and Human Services uses "patient care episodes" to estimate the number of people treated each year for mental illness. This metric tracks the number of people treated at psychiatric hospitals, residential facilities for the mentally ill, and ambulatory care facilities. In 1955 the government reported 1,675,352 patient care episodes, or 1,028 episodes per 100,000 population. In 2000, patient care episodes totaled 10,741,243, or 3,806 per 100,000 persons—nearly a fourfold increase per capita in fifty years, as shown in Table 4.1.

A second way to assess this epidemic is to look at the number of mentally ill people who require government assistance. Until the 1950s, the number of hospitalized mentally ill provided a rough estimate of this group. Today the disabled mentally ill typically receive a disability payment either from the Social Security Disability Insurance (SSDI) program or the Supplemental Security Income (SSI) program, and many live in residential shelters or other subsidized living arrangements. Thus, the hospitalized patient of fifty years ago today receives either SSDI or SSI, and this line of evidence reveals that the number of disabled mentally ill has increased nearly sixfold since chlorpromazine was introduced.

In 1955 there were 559,000 people in public mental hospitals, or 3.38 persons per 1,000 population. In 2004 5.875 million people received either an SSI or SSDI payment (or received a payment from both programs), and were either disabled by mental illness (SSDI statistics) or

Table 4.2 The Disabled Mentally Ill in the United States

Year	Rate of Disabled Mentally Ill Persons Per 1,000 Population
1850	0.2*
1903	1.86*
1955	3.38*
1987	13.75†
2004	20.58†

Source: Data provided by E. F. Torrey and the U.S. Social Security Administration.

* Rates for 1850, 1903, and 1955 are based on the number of hospitalized mentally ill cited by Torrey, E. F. (2001). *The Invisible Plague: The Rise of Mental Illness from 1750 to the Present.* New Brunswick, NJ: Rutgers University Press.

† The disability rates for 1987 and 2004 are based on the number of mentally ill persons receiving SSI or SSDI payments, as reported by the U.S. Social Security Administration in 2005.

diagnosed as mentally ill (SSI statistics). As shown in Table 4.2, this correlates to a disability rate of 20.58 persons per 1,000 population, nearly six times greater than the rate in 1955.

It is also noteworthy that the number of disabled mentally ill has increased dramatically since 1987, the year Prozac was introduced. From 1987 through 2004, the number of disabled mentally ill in the United States, as calculated by the SSI and SSDI figures, increased from 3.331 million to 5.875 million people.[17] This is an increase of 149,647 people per year, or 410 people newly disabled by mental illness every day, as shown in Table 4.3.

Table 4.3 Disability in the Prozac Era

Year	SSDI Recipients Disabled by Mental Illness	SSI Recipients with Diagnosis of Mental Illness	Total No. of SSI and SSDI Recipients Disabled by Mental Illness	No. of SSDI Recipients Who Also Received an SSI Payment	Total Disabled Mentally Ill
1987	800,139	2,630,999	3,431,138	(100,017)	3,331,121
2004	1,922,907	4,192,707	6,115,614	(240,362)	5,875,252

Source: Data from the 2004 Annual Statistical Report on the Social Security Disability Insurance program and the 2004 Annual Statistical Report on the Social Security Supplemental Security Income program.

Creating Bipolar Children and Adolescents

The emergence over the past fifteen years of juvenile bipolar disorder as a common ailment has unfolded against this larger backdrop. So as we investigate whether our drug-based paradigm of care may be contributing to the pediatric bipolar epidemic, we need to remember these four facts:

1. Children and adolescents who are diagnosed with mental disorders have no known chemical imbalance in the brain.
2. Once diagnosed, they are regularly prescribed psychiatric drugs that perturb normal neurotransmitter function, and as a result of that perturbation, their brains operate in an abnormal manner.
3. We should expect such perturbation of normal neurotransmitter function to stir up new and more severe psychiatric symptoms—or, as E. Fuller Torrey describes them, the "symptoms of insanity"—in a significant percentage of the youths so treated.
4. In adults, this paradigm of care has led to an astonishing increase in the number of disabled mentally ill, evidence of how the drugs can be disease-causing agents.

The Rise of Juvenile Bipolar Disorder

At the dawn of the psychopharmacology era (the 1950s), psychiatric researchers regularly reported that manic-depressive illness in children was extremely rare.[18] In 1950 Lurie concluded that it simply didn't occur in childhood.[19] Two years later Hall reviewed the case histories of 2,200 child and adolescent psychiatric patients treated over the previous decades and identified only two cases of manic-depressive illness, both in patients over age thirteen.[20] All of this led Anthony to conclude in 1960 that "occurrence of manic depression in early childhood as a clinical phenomenon has yet to be demonstrated."[21]

This belief continued into the 1970s, and then a handful of psychiatrists began to make clinical observations of bipolar symptoms in a few of their pediatric patients. In 1976, Weinberg recommended new criteria—based on those proposed for adult mania—for diagnosing the disorder in children,[22] and both DeLong[23] and Davis[24] echoed this theme. And then in the 1990s, that trickle of early-onset bipolar disorder in children and adolescents turned into a torrent. In 1995 Lewinsohn announced that 1 percent of all adolescents had bipolar disorder (BD), and that nearly 6 percent had subthreshold BD symptoms.[25] That same year Faedda and others pronounced juvenile bipolar disorder a "neglected clinical and public health problem."[26] A *Parents of Bipolar Children* Web site appeared on the Internet, and in 2000 Demitri Papolos, research director of the Juvenile Bipolar Research Foundation, coauthored a popular book titled *The Bipolar Child* with his wife Janice Papolos. "Bipolar disorder was once thought to be rare in childhood," he told his readers. "Now researchers are discovering that not only can bipolar disorder begin very early in life but also that it is much more common than ever imagined."[27] Finally, in August 2002, in an article titled "Young and Bipolar," *Time* magazine reported that "experts estimate that one million preteens and children in the U.S. may suffer from the early stages of bipolar disorder."[28]

What was the cause of the appearance of this disorder? *Time* said that it could be explained in part by a "new awareness of the disorder," implying that doctors and parents had previously been blind to the fact that many children were cycling between depressed and manic states. Yet the magazine also confessed that even that explanation "may not be enough to account for the explosion of juvenile bipolar cases. Some scientists fear there may be something in the environment or in modern lifestyles that is driving into a bipolar state children and teens who might otherwise escape the condition."

This latter explanation—that there is something in the environment causing the emergence of this disorder—has an obvious scientific rationale. If bipolar disorder in children and adolescents is indeed real, and if 1 percent of all youth are truly exhibiting these symptoms that doctors fifty years ago said they almost never saw, then it would make sense to look for a disease-causing agent to explain the emergence of this disorder. And based on the observed history of this disorder, it would seem that this disease-causing agent first began to "infect" children in the late 1960s and early 1970s, prompting Weinberg, DeLong, and Davis to argue that juvenile bipolar disorder was real and ought to be recognized by clinicians. Then, starting in the late 1980s, this disease-causing agent apparently spread and multiplied, infecting more and more children, such that by 2000 Dr. Papolos could confidently publish a book titled *The Bipolar Child*, and experts in the field would tell *Time* magazine that an estimated one million children and adolescents suffered from the disorder.

The search for such disease-causing agents leads to two possible culprits: the stimulants used to treat ADHD, and SSRI antidepressants. A review of the scientific literature reveals that these drugs are indeed contributing to this "epidemic" of juvenile bipolar disorder.

The ADHD Gateway to Bipolar Illness

Ritalin, which is the trade name for methylphenidate, was marketed by Ciba Pharmaceuticals in 1956 as a treatment for drug-induced lethargy, mild depression, and narcolepsy. During the 1960s, some psychiatrists began prescribing it to children who were overactive or had other behavioral problems, and by 1970 an estimated 150,000 children and adolescents were taking the drug.[29] The matching of Ritalin to a "disease" then took a big step forward in 1980, when the American Psychiatric Association (APA) used the term "attention deficit disorder" for the first time in the third edition of its *Diagnostic and Statistical Manual of Mental Disorders (DSM-III)*. Finally came the 1987 publication of a revised edition of the *DSM-III-R* that introduced the term "attention deficit hyperactive disorder" for the first time. The cardinal symptoms of this disorder are "inattention, hyperactivity, and impulsivity."

By the mid-1980s, perhaps as many as 500,000 children and adolescents in the United States were being prescribed Ritalin, with the Drug Enforcement Administration (DEA) reporting that 1,361 kilograms of methylphenidate were produced that year for U.S. consumption.[30] But with the APA having officially identified ADHD as a disease in 1987, Ritalin prescriptions began to soar. Between 1985 and 1995, production of methylphenidate for use in the United States jumped eightfold, to 10,410 kilograms.[31] A second drug for ADHD, an amphetamine (Adderall), was brought to market in 1996, and by 2002, there were an estimated three to five million Americans under age twenty on an ADHD medication.

Even at first glance, it is easy to see a striking overlap in the use of methylphenidate and the emerging awareness of juvenile bipolar disorder. Psychiatry's recognition of this "illness" rose in lockstep with soaring rates of stimulant prescriptions. Furthermore, the disease-causing process associated with these drugs is easily outlined. Children diagnosed with ADHD have no known biological abnormality. However, after being treated with Ritalin or one of the other ADHD drugs, they do. Their brains, as Steve Hyman explained, end up functioning in a manner that is "qualitatively and quantitatively" different than normal, and as a result—as the scientific literature shows—many exhibit symptoms that lead to a diagnosis of juvenile bipolar disorder.

Methylphenidate is a stimulant that blocks the reuptake of dopamine from the synaptic cleft and thus is said to boost dopamine levels in the brain. (Amphetamines increase dopamine levels by stimulating the release of dopamine.) Cocaine also blocks the reuptake of dopamine from the synaptic cleft, and researchers have reported that methylphenidate's potency is equivalent to that of cocaine.[32] The principal difference between the two drugs is that cocaine, when snorted, boosts dopamine levels much more quickly than a methylphenidate tablet does, and cocaine clears from the brain more quickly as well. This quick rush of dopamine is what provides cocaine users with a high, and its quick clearance is what makes the drug addictive. Methylphenidate (in pill form) provides for a more gradual and sustained blocking of the normal reuptake of dopamine in the brain.

In response to the drug's perturbation of dopamine function, the brain tries to compensate by toning down its dopaminergic system. The density of dopamine receptors in the brain decreases (or, as some psychiatric researchers prefer to put it, the density of dopamine receptors is "down-regulated"), and this change is part of the larger cascade of compensatory changes described by Hyman in his 1996 paper.

Children prescribed methylphenidate and other ADHD drugs experience a spectrum of behavioral and mental changes, some of which are deemed therapeutic and others which are chalked up as "adverse events." [33] These drug-induced changes may be broadly grouped into two types—arousal and dysphoric symptoms—as listed in the following:

Arousal	**Dysphoric**
Increased energy	Somnolence
Intensified focus	Fatigue, lethargy
Hyperalertness	Social withdrawal and isolation
Euphoria	Decreased spontaneity
Agitation, anxiety, nervousness	Reduced curiosity
Insomnia	Constriction of affect
Irritability	Depression
Hostility	Apathy
Obsessive-compulsive behaviors	Emotional lability
Hypomania	
Mania	
Psychosis	

Drug-induced changes such as intensified focus, constriction of affect, and social withdrawal may be viewed as helpful and therapeutic for a child who is fidgety and inattentive in school. The child may become more focused on her work and interact less with peers, and thus become less disruptive. However, it is easy to see that a child treated with an ADHD medication may cycle through arousal and dysphoric states (a cycle that may be related at least in part to changing levels of methylphenidate in the brain), and it is to be expected that some children will experience the more severe adverse events, such as mania and psychosis.[34]

It is easy to see how the spectrum of symptoms induced by ADHD drugs overlap with the symptoms that lead to a diagnosis of juvenile bipolar disorder. According to the National Institute of Mental Health,[35] the characteristic symptoms of juvenile bipolar disorder—grouped here into arousal and dysphoric categories—are these:

Arousal	Dysphoric
Increased energy	Sad mood
Intensified goal-directed activity	Loss of energy
Decreased need for sleep	Loss of interest in activities
Severe changes in mood	Social isolation
Irritability	Poor communication
Physical agitation	Feelings of worthlessness
Destructive outbursts	Unexplained crying
Increased talking	
Distractibility	
Grandiosity	

The progression from ADHD to juvenile bipolar disorder is also well recognized by ADHD experts, even though they refrain from concluding that the drugs cause it. For example, in a pamphlet titled "Bipolar Affective Disorder in Children and Adolescents," Dr. James Chandler warns that "over 90 percent of children who get manic had ADHD before they got manic or hypomanic."[36] The National Alliance for the Mentally Ill advises parents "ADHD often appears before a clear development of the alternating mood swings and prolonged temper tantrums associated with child-onset bipolar disorder."[37] *Time* magazine told readers that children diagnosed with bipolar disorder are usually diagnosed with another psychiatric disorder first, with "ADHD the likeliest first call."[38] And in 1996, Biederman reported that 12 percent of ADHD children who did not have bipolar symptoms at initial diagnosis went on to develop bipolar disorder within four years.[39]

The critical question then is this: Would 12 percent of all children and adolescents diagnosed with ADHD—and determined at the moment of initial diagnosis not to suffer from bipolar disorder—progress to a bipolar diagnosis if they weren't treated with Ritalin or some other ADHD medication? The available evidence shows that a much smaller percentage would follow this course if they weren't treated with ADHD medications. Consider the following:

1. Prior to the 1950s, psychiatrists reported that they almost never saw manic-depressive illness in children. Thus, before the use of these drugs, hyperactive children did not regularly worsen and suffer

manic episodes (or the other symptoms on which diagnosis of juvenile bipolar disorder is based).

2. In 2001 Dutch researchers reported that although 39 percent of U.S.
adolescents with a bipolar parent develop bipolar disorder before age
twenty, only 4 percent of Dutch children do. Thus, U.S. children in this
at-risk group were *ten times* more likely to develop juvenile bipolar
disorder than their Dutch counterparts, and the researchers concluded that this "huge difference" was likely due to "the much higher
use of stimulants as well as antidepressants by U.S. children."[40]

3. The drug-induced explanation for the emergence of juvenile bipolar
disorder follows the logic of a classical model of disease. An outside
agent enters the system, disturbs normal function, and causes various symptoms. This is precisely what has happened in this iatrogenic
disease: Methylphenidate (or another ADHD drug) is the outside
agent. It perturbs the dopaminergic system, causing a host of physical and mental symptoms, and 12 percent of children who are without bipolar symptoms at initial diagnosis subsequently develop this
more severe condition.

This is not to say that all children diagnosed with juvenile bipolar
disorder are first diagnosed with ADHD and then develop bipolar
symptoms after being treated with ADHD medications. But it does
suggest that this is a primary iatrogenic pathway to juvenile bipolar
disorder. There is a second such iatrogenic pathway as well: treatment
of depressive episodes in children with an SSRI antidepressant.

The SSRI Pathway to Bipolar Illness

In 1987 Eli Lilly introduced to the public the first SSRI
antidepressant—fluoxetine, marketed as Prozac—with the claim that
it was safer and more effective than the older line of tricyclic antidepressants. As a result psychiatrists began prescribing it to children
with great frequency. The number of such prescriptions rose rapidly
and steadily for the next fifteen years, so that by 2002 an estimated two
million American children were taking antidepressants.[41]

As noted earlier in this chapter, SSRI antidepressants block the
normal reuptake of serotonin in the brain—to an extent termed
"pathologic" by Princeton neuroscientist Barry Jacob. Perhaps not surprisingly, in Prozac's first two years on the market, the FDA's Medwatch program received more adverse-event reports about this new
"wonder drug" than it had received for the leading tricyclic antidepressant of the previous twenty years. Prozac quickly took the top
position as America's most complained about drug, and by 1997
39,000 adverse-event reports about it had been sent to Medwatch.
These reports are thought to represent only 1 percent of the actual

number of such events, suggesting that as a consequence of taking Prozac, nearly four million people in the United States suffered such problems as mania, psychotic depression, nervousness, anxiety, agitation, hostility, hallucinations, memory loss, tremors, impotence, convulsions, insomnia, and nausea. The other SSRIs brought to market caused a similar range of problems.[42]

Slightly more than 1 percent of Prozac patients in the clinical trials developed mania.[43] Subsequent studies found much higher rates of SSRI-induced mania. In 1996 Howland reported that 6 percent of 184 depressed patients treated with an SSRI suffered manic episodes that were "generally quite severe."[44] A year later Ebert reported that 8.5 percent of patients had a severe psychological reaction to Luvox (fluvoxamine).[45] Robert Bourguignon, after surveying doctors in Belgium, estimated that Prozac induced psychotic episodes in 5 to 7 percent of patients.[46]

Although the studies cited above looked at SSRI-induced mania or psychosis in adults, studies with children documented the same risk. Jain reported that 23 percent of boys eight to nineteen years old treated with Prozac developed mania or maniclike symptoms, and another 19 percent developed "drug-induced" hostility.[47] Yet another study of Prozac determined that the drug triggered mania in 6 percent of depressed children aged seven to seventeen, whereas none of the depressed children who took a placebo suffered a manic episode.[48] Similarly, Luvox was reported to cause a 4 percent rate of mania in children under eighteen.[49] And in 2004, the FDA concluded that SSRI antidepressants stir suicidal thoughts in 2 to 3 percent of all children.[50]

Given the risk of drug-induced mania, psychosis, and suicidal ideation, it is to be expected that many children treated with an SSRI will go on to be diagnosed with juvenile bipolar disorder, and this is indeed the case. In their 1995 paper, Faedda and colleagues concluded that 25 percent of depressed children treated with antidepressants eventually develop mania or hypomania and thus progress to a bipolar diagnosis. They wrote: "Antidepressant treatment may well induce switching into mania, rapid cycling or affective instability in the young, as it almost certainly does in adults. This possibility evidently brings special risks to the use of stimulants and antidepressants."[51] The American Academy of Child and Adolescent Psychiatry now warns that 20 to 30 percent of all children initially diagnosed with major depression will go on to have manic episodes.[52]

The critical question is this: What percentage of children diagnosed with depression would progress to a bipolar diagnosis if they were never treated with antidepressants? Faedda and colleagues concluded that the spontaneous switching rate is unknown, and thus "the difference between antidepressant-associated and spontaneous switching into mania or hypomania from depression is not well quantified in adult or pediatric mood-disordered populations." However, the studies I have cited reveal that the drugs triggered mania in 4 to 19 percent of all children in research trials that often lasted only six weeks or so. The rate of drug-induced switching over a period of several years could be expected to be much higher. In addition, the same historical backdrop applies here as it does in the case of ADHD drugs: Prior to the 1950s, psychiatrists weren't reporting that depressed children were progressing to manic-depressive illness. This is a new phenomenon that only appeared in the 1990s, just as SSRI antidepressant drug prescriptions were becoming widespread.

In summary, the scientific literature reveals two iatrogenic pathways to juvenile bipolar disorder. Furthermore, parents of bipolar children bear witness to this fact. In May 1999 Martha Hellander, executive director of the Child and Adolescent Bipolar Foundation, and Tomie Burke, founder of Parents of Bipolar Children, wrote in a letter to the editor of the *Journal of the American Academy of Child and Adolescent Psychiatry* that "most of our children initially received the ADHD diagnosis, were given stimulants and/or antidepressants, and either did not respond or [responded with] symptoms of mania such as rages, insomnia, agitation, pressured speech, and the like. In lay language, parents call this 'bouncing off the wall.' First hospitalization occurred often among our children during manic or mixed states (including suicidal gestures and attempts) triggered or exacerbated by treatment with stimulants, tricyclics, or selective serotonin reuptake inhibitors."[53]

In other words, parents tell again and again of an iatrogenic disease process that led to their children being diagnosed as bipolar.

Setting the Stage for a Life as a Psychiatric Patient

The tragedy of this iatrogenic process is that it may inflict permanent harm on the child. Once a child is diagnosed with bipolar disorder, he or she is typically treated with a drug cocktail that includes both an atypical antipsychotic and a mood stabilizer. One study of bipolar children found that more than half were taking at least three psychotropic medications.[54] And once a child is on a drug cocktail that contains an antipsychotic, he is well on his way to a muted and shortened life as a psychiatric patient. The cocktail will profoundly perturb the normal functioning of a child's brain and alter its development as well. As a result the child will suffer a host of physical and psychiatric symptoms. Not surprisingly experts in this field now

Table 4.4 Pity the Children (Total Who Receive SSI for Severe Mental Illness)

Year	Under 5 Years	5–12 Years Old	13–17 Years Old	Total (Birth–17 Years Old)
2000	22,543	146,184	130,415	258,820
2001	23,677	167,379	105,738	296,794
2002	27,991	189,140	122,389	339,520
2003	31,542	214,139	141,854	387,535
2004	35,164	235,919	162,863	433,946

warn that those diagnosed with juvenile bipolar disorder face a dismal future (although they don't blame the drugs for it). "Prepubertal mania may follow a chronic course, characterized by high rates of relapse, psychiatric hospitalizations, chronicity, and the need for several medications," warns a Web site associated with the American Academy of Pediatrics.[55] Chandler tells his patients the same: "Pediatric bipolar illness is very severe and chronic."[56]

We have thus adopted a paradigm of care that can transform a child who is inattentive or fidgety in school into a person who is chronically ill with bipolar disorder and in apparent need of lifelong antipsychotic treatment. This paradigm of care can have the same results for a child who slips into a depressive episode. And just as our drug-based paradigm of care is producing an ever-increasing number of disabled mentally ill adults, it is now also producing an ever-increasing number of disabled mentally ill children. Indeed, prescribing antipsychotics to children serves as a rough marker for the number of disabled mentally ill children created in the past fifteen years, because such powerful drugs are reserved—at least in theory—for the severely disturbed. In 1993 antipsychotic medications were prescribed to 0.275 percent of all children in the United States, or to about 201,000 children between birth and twenty years of age. In 2002 antipsychotics were prescribed to 1.438 percent of all children, or to about 1,224,000 children and adolescents.[57] This is an increase of 102,300 children per year over a span of ten years, or 280 children newly medicated with an antipsychotic every day.

Federal SSI data tell a similarly heartbreaking story. In 1985, at the start of the ADHD boom, 18,410 children under age eighteen received supplemental security payments because they were severely mentally ill. Over the course of the next two decades, as children were increasingly prescribed drugs for ADHD and depression, the number of children receiving SSI payments because of severe mental illness increased to 433,946, as shown in Table 4.4. The number of children so disabled by mental illness continues to soar: in 2004 alone, 96,270 children were added to the SSI rolls because they were disabled by mental illness.

Those cold statistics tell of harm done on an almost unfathomable scale.

5

The Childhood Bipolar Epidemic: Brat or Bipolar?

Elizabeth J. Roberts

CHILDHOOD BIPOLAR DISORDER: THE NEW "DIAGNOSIS DU JOUR"

Psychiatric diagnoses go through phases of popularity. This was definitely the case in the 1970s with the diagnosis of multiple personality disorder (MPD). MPD was so popular that it became the subject of many best-selling books and blockbuster movies such as *The Three Faces of Eve* and *Sybil*. In the years that followed its peak popularity, doctors and therapists became painfully aware that they had over-diagnosed MPD to the point that it is no longer even included in psychiatry's most recent version of the *Diagnostic and Statistical Manual* (*DSM-IV-TR*). It has been replaced by dissociative identity disorder (DID), a condition that is rarely diagnosed.[1]

Children's psychiatric diagnoses also wax and wane in popularity. Attention-deficit/hyperactivity disorder (ADHD) first became trendy in the 1980s. In order to appreciate the full extent of the ADHD fervor, one need only examine the number of prescriptions written for this condition. Medications such as Ritalin, Adderall, Concerta, and Metadate are amphetamines, a class of drugs that is primarily prescribed for the ADHD diagnosis. According to the Drug Enforcement Administration (DEA), the number of prescriptions for amphetamines rose by 500 percent between 1991 and 2000.[2] Prior to 1980, ADHD was a little-known disorder, but by 2006, this diagnosis had become so popular that fully 10 percent of all ten-year-old boys in the United States were being medicated with amphetamines.[3]

The most recent "diagnosis du jour" in children is bipolar disorder (BD). Over the past decade, there has been an explosive rise in the number of children being diagnosed with this illness. This is a particularly disturbing development in psychiatry because children who receive this diagnosis are typically prescribed antipsychotic drugs that are fraught with dangerous side effects. These are the same powerful drugs used to treat adults with schizophrenia. Between 1995 and 2002, there was an unprecedented, fivefold increase in antipsychotic prescriptions for children, which translates into a leap from 275 to 1,438 prescriptions per 100,000 children in a seven-year period.[4] Dr. Cooper at Vanderbilt Children's Hospital estimated that 2.5 million children were taking antipsychotic drugs in 2006.[5] Antipsychotics are generally prescribed to children for a diagnosis of bipolar disorder.

Overmedicating children in the name of bipolar disorder is part of a wider trend in child psychiatry. Three times as many children are taking psychiatric medication today, compared to only fifteen years ago.[6] According to the U.S. Centers for Disease Control and Prevention, almost 20 percent of office visits to pediatricians are for psychological problems, eclipsing both asthma and heart disease.[7] As a result minors are starting to outpace the elderly in the consumption of pharmaceuticals.[8]

These statistics obligate us to examine why millions of children are being prescribed increasingly potent and dangerous psychiatric drugs. The meteoric rise in the number of children being diagnosed with bipolar disorder cannot be traced to a single source. This epidemic was fomented by several different forces that have converged to create the conditions for a perfect storm. Overzealous parents, hurried doctors, and misinformed teachers are all part of a complex system that is driving this contemporary obsession of diagnosing children with bipolar disorder.

THE DIRE CONSEQUENCES OF MISDIAGNOSIS

Bipolar disorder is now diagnosed so casually that any child whose symptoms include irritation, anger, frustration, insomnia, sadness, or aggression is likely to be labeled bipolar in spite of the fact that there are many reasons that children might feel this way. Frightened, bullied, abused, and grieving children, as well as kids making adjustments to new situations such as divorce, would be expected to exhibit any or all of these symptoms. Although some children actually do have bipolar disorder, many others are incorrectly diagnosed when they in fact suffer from an entirely different condition. Unfortunately, children whose symptoms more closely meet the criteria for other disorders, such as adjustment disorder, major depressive disorder, anxiety disorder, post-traumatic stress disorder, intermittent explosive disorder, or oppositional defiant disorder, nonetheless are being carelessly tagged with the "bipolar" moniker. To make matters worse, many clinicians believe that bipolar children require nothing more than medication. Consequently, once children are given this diagnosis, medicine is often the only treatment provided, posing a formidable barrier to appropriate interventions and therapies.

Although this scenario is already disturbing, perhaps the most reprehensible misuse of this popular psychiatric diagnosis is its application to ordinary belligerent children. Parents, teachers, and clinicians now frequently characterize the typical defiance, misbehavior, and temper tantrums of bratty children as bipolar disorder. Doctors are using the bipolar diagnosis to justify sedating these difficult children with powerful psychiatric drugs—drugs that have serious, permanent, and sometimes lethal side effects.[9]

As I describe in my book *Should You Medicate Your Child's Mind?*, initiating treatment based on the wrong diagnosis usually leads to the use of medications when they are completely unwarranted, or to prescribing the wrong medications. Misdiagnosed children on the wrong prescription drugs generally do not get better. Tragically, when children's symptoms continue unchanged or perhaps even worsen, the psychiatrist usually assumes that the medications, not the diagnosis, need to be adjusted. Rarely do child psychiatrists consider the possibility that the bipolar diagnosis was wrong to begin with. Instead they typically adjust the treatment by adding one or more medications to those already prescribed. And so the misdiagnosis of bipolar disorder launches the child on a treacherous journey toward overmedication and away from effective care.

THE PERSPECTIVES OF PARENTS, PSYCHIATRISTS, AND TEACHERS

Parents, mental health professionals, and teachers each have their own unique insights into the emotional world and behaviors of children. Taken together, the experiences and perspectives of these three groups provide a more complete understanding of childhood. Because I have successfully raised my own children to adulthood, worked as a schoolteacher in the best and worst of neighborhoods, and worked more recently as a psychiatrist with both disadvantaged and privileged children, I am privy to this integrated understanding of children's mental health. Unfortunately though, parents, psychiatrists, and teachers, for different reasons, have also played significant roles in fomenting the pediatric bipolar epidemic.

Parents and the Pediatric Bipolar Epidemic:
A Spoiling Crisis in America

Children require a host of skills to function as adults. These skills include the ability to accept *frustration* as a part of life, to manage disappointments, and to muster the self-control to delay gratification and make mature choices. Unfortunately, the discipline of children has been relegated to a position of minimal importance by our society. Dan Kindlon, a Harvard University psychologist, found that 50 percent of the parents he interviewed described themselves as more permissive than their own parents had been.[10] And in a recent poll, 93 percent of people surveyed stated that today's parents are not doing a good job when it comes to teaching their kids to behave. When children's every whim is indulged and they are placated whenever they are the least bit frustrated, they do not learn how to function successfully either in adolescence or adulthood. In the current climate, the consequences of spoiling go well beyond creating a monster for the family, school, and neighborhood to deal with. A spoiled child who rages at the least disappointment is now at significant risk for a misdiagnosis of bipolar disorder and an antipsychotic drug prescription.

One of the reasons that undisciplined, out-of-control kids are likely to receive a psychiatric diagnosis is that it has become taboo for child psychiatrists to suggest that parents are in any way responsible for their children's difficult behaviors. From the 1940s through the 1970s when psychoanalytic approaches dominated psychiatry, therapists tended to blame mothers for their children's psychological disturbances. Over the past few decades, the pendulum has swung too far in the other direction. Now it is politically incorrect for psychiatrists to even intimate that parents are in any way responsible for their children's negative behaviors. The temper tantrums and classroom disruptions of defiant children are now defined exclusively as chemical imbalances and neurotransmitter deficits. Psychiatrists who challenge this conventional thinking are dismissed as being "old school" and out of touch with current practices. But those of us who do speak out are saying "the emperor has no clothes."

Parents today have so much information at their fingertips that they often feel qualified to diagnose their children and then demand a prescription for a drug of their own choosing. They know that if the first doctor doesn't prescribe what they want, the next one will.[11] Time-pressured doctors working within the constraints of a health maintenance organization are often all too willing to accept without question the assessment offered by the parent. Unfortunately, parents' research is often gleaned from Web sites, magazine ads and articles, and self-administered surveys. Web sites and articles provide little more than partial or completely incorrect information; they certainly cannot replace the thorough evaluation of a trained professional. Descriptions on the Internet often downplay the seriousness of various psychiatric conditions and the dangerous side effects of many psychiatric drugs. For parents, what was once a somber, heart-wrenching decision—putting their child on a psychiatric medication—has now become a widely used technique for dealing with an unruly child. As if they were debating parental locks on the home computer or coed sleepovers, parents now share notes with each other about whose kid is taking what pill for which diagnosis.

To complicate matters, parents frequently misuse medical jargon that they have gleaned from the media. Doctors do not realize that when parents use the term mood swings, they mean that their children are nitpicky, irritable, cranky, fussy, or grumpy. Parents may also apply this term to a child who cries or flies into a rage when he is denied what he wants but then recovers just as quickly once he gets his way. Most children who refuse to cooperate, defy rules, and have temper tantrums when things don't go their way have not been taught to respect their teachers and parents or to follow rules. By contrast, the *Diagnostic and Statistical Manual of Mental Disorders* defines "mood swings" as intermittent episodes of mania and depression.[12] When this term for a key symptom of bipolar disorder is casually bandied about by a parent and the physician doesn't take the time to find out what the term means to the parent, the stage is set for a misdiagnosis and a drug prescription.

In summary, in an era of permissive parenting, far more children exhibit behavior that is out of control. At the same time, current attitudes in child psychiatry encourage physicians to explain all of a child's disruptive behavior as resulting exclusively from faulty brain chemistry rather than from poor parenting. For many parents it is a relief to be told that their child's defiant, belligerent, and aggressive behavior is the result of a psychiatric condition and therefore not the fault or responsibility of their ineffective childrearing.

Psychiatrists and the Pediatric Bipolar Epidemic

Some psychiatrists speculate that the stunning increase in the number of children diagnosed with bipolar disorder is entirely the result of improved diagnostic techniques. However, many psychiatrists believe that diagnoses of bipolar disorder are frequently used as

a justification to medicate a child's mind as a quick-fix convenience for educators, doctors, and parents alike. As a consequence, ordinary bratty behaviors are being attributed to a chemical imbalance, and children are being medicated inappropriately just to quiet them down. Many clinicians find it easier to tell parents that their child has a brain-based disorder than to suggest parenting changes.[13]

A common pathway to misdiagnosis is when a psychiatrist does not take the time to understand the child's problems thoroughly. Here is an example of how a doctor might arrive at the wrong diagnosis, based on incomplete information. A boy who is easily angered, loses his temper when he doesn't get his way, and refuses to do his chores and home-work is brought to a psychiatrist for a consultation. He is oppositional, defies the rules at school and at home, and argues with the teacher and his parents. He ignores his parents regarding his bedtime and stays up late playing video games. In class he purposely antagonizes his teacher by clowning around and leaving his assigned seat to interfere with his classmates' studies simply for its entertainment value.

An accurate diagnosis of a child with these symptoms would be oppositional defiant disorder (ODD). But imagine that the doctor only learned that the child was not doing his work and often left his class-room seat. He might then conclude that the child had ADHD. For the diagnosis of ADHD, doctors usually prescribe amphetamines, which would indeed help the child do his homework more efficiently. Of course, amphetamines would help anyone concentrate and focus bet-ter, regardless of whether they had ADHD. On the other hand, if the child did not *want* to comply, he might still refuse to do any of his schoolwork, continue to antagonize his teacher, argue with adults, and behave defiantly, even when he was medicated.

Now consider how the diagnosis might change for this same child when the parent reports only that the boy is easily angered, has tantrums, is not sleeping at night, and clowns around in class. Then the psychiatrist might conclude that he has bipolar disorder. For this diag-nosis doctors usually prescribe powerful psychotropic drugs, such as mood-stabilizing medications and antipsychotics. These drugs would certainly help sedate the boy—he would definitely be sleeping well after a dose of these medications. Overall he would appear more calm and less angry and agitated. These mood-stabilizers and antipsychotics have the power to calm any child regardless of his or her psychiatric diagno-sis. Yet when sedating a boy causes him to be even a little less unruly, the doctor will see this response as confirmation of the diagnosis of bipolar disorder. Nonetheless, a sedated child is not necessarily a more compli-ant child. Although he may not be more cooperative when he is sedated, he certainly will make less noise and create less chaos in the classroom.

When a child is misdiagnosed, their actual problems are not properly addressed. Oppositional defiant disorder is caused by permissive parenting and should not be treated with medications at all. The treatment for ODD consists of educating parents in order to help them learn behavioral management techniques that stop their children's belligerent behaviors. However, when a diagnosis is rushed, and psychotropic medications are hastily prescribed, parents never receive the proper advice on how to manage their ODD child. Without behavioral intervention, the child will likely receive more drugs and different drugs in an attempt to control each symptom that did not respond to the original medications. What a horrifying prospect—but it happens every day in the practice of child psychiatry, all for the want of effective communication and a thoughtful evaluation. Getting the diagnosis right is essential to receiving the proper treatment. Otherwise doctors will continue to medicate children needlessly.[14]

Even more egregious and worrisome than the current diagnostic practices of child psychiatrists are efforts on the part of the American Academy of Child and Adolescent Psychiatry (AACAP) to craft new diagnostic criteria for pediatric bipolar disorder. Child psychiatrists already stretch and distort the existing criteria in order to justify diagnosing belligerent children who throw temper tantrums with this condition. However, if AACAP's proposed guidelines for childhood bipolar disorder are adopted by the *DSM* editorial staff, many more children would actually fit the criteria for the diagnosis of bipolar disorder. In AACAP's proposed practice parameters for assessing pediatric bipolar disorder, mania has been redefined as belligerence, irritability, anger, explosiveness, and dysphoria. The guidelines also state that most bipolar children do not always have discrete episodes of depression and mania, but are simply cranky and ornery all of the time, and to the extent that they do have discrete manic episodes, the episodes may last just minutes as opposed to weeks and may resolve as soon as the child gets her way. If AACAP succeeds in its bid to have their criteria for childhood bipolar disorder included in the next edition of the *DSM*, psychiatrists will have justified years of misdiagnosing and overmedicating children, and this dangerous trend will continue with a vengeance.[15]

Teachers and the Pediatric Bipolar Epidemic: Cost-Effective Classroom Management

Public schools operate on a tight budget. The amount of money that is actually allocated for instruction is limited indeed. Furthermore, public schools are mandated to provide an education to all children, regardless of their physical and mental challenges. Therefore, when an avenue can be found for dealing with a student's academic or behavioral problems that does not cut into their budget, many school administrators are relieved to exercise that option. For each student who has been identified with a psychiatric condition, the school receives extra funds from the state and federal governments. However, if a child is offered nothing more than psychiatric medications that will likely be paid for through her parents' medical insurance, then the school can redirect those extra funds into its general education budget. So when a child receives a psychiatric diagnosis and is treated exclusively with medication, not only is the school not required to cover the cost of his treatment, but it also actually gains financially.

By contrast, when teachers advocate for their students to receive the extra services that special education provides—such as speech therapy, one-on-one aides in the classroom, or special equipment to accommodate the students' learning disabilities—they often run into resistance. Many administrators, struggling to make ends meet with their already stretched budgets, discourage teachers from recommending special education services to families, even when they are the most appropriate interventions. Some teachers have even been threatened with the loss of their jobs if they inform students and their parents about the special education services to which the children are entitled. This leads to a disproportionate number of families being encouraged to seek psychiatric medications for their children who may simply have academic difficulties. Rather than offering families the alternative, safer and more appropriate classroom interventions that would cut into the school's budget, administrators prefer parents to address their children's behavioral problems at the doctor's office.

I worked as a public and private schoolteacher for several years before attending medical school. I am acutely aware of the important role teachers play in guiding and protecting children. This said, teachers are not doctors. Although teachers may be very useful in identifying behavioral issues, they are not medically qualified to diagnose psychiatric disorders and should certainly not advocate for the use of any specific medications. Too often parents have reported to me that their child's teacher has said something like, "I think Johnnie has bipolar disorder. You should think about taking him to see a psychiatrist for some medication." Unfortunately, many teachers feel very comfortable diagnosing their students with any number of psychiatric illnesses, including bipolar disorder. These teachers present themselves to their students' parents as mental health experts based on their many years in the classroom, their personal struggles with the same disorder, or their experience with their own child who has a mental illness. But experience with psychologically disturbed children in the classroom or home does not replace a medical degree.[16]

For some teachers—especially those struggling with large class sizes—classroom management rather than students' welfare is their first priority. They may worry that if their students are out of control, their colleagues will view this as evidence of their weak instructional skills. It only takes one or two students provoking the rest of the students to laughter to give the appearance that the entire classroom is in chaos. But if the troublemaking student can be pegged with a mental illness, the teacher cannot be held responsible for the disruption in her classroom. Subduing a disruptive child with psychiatric drugs is one way a teacher can avoid the shame of appearing to be ineffective. Of course, children may then be unnecessarily medicated.[17] As a result, if a child is unruly and disruptive in the classroom, his parents may come under pressure from his teacher to have him medicated. And when a teacher pressures parents to place their child on medications, the parents often pressure their doctor to write a prescription.

Parents can be easily intimidated when their child's teacher or principal threatens to expel their child if psychiatric medications are not prescribed. Remember, if a school can convince a family to medicate a student to address his disruptive behaviors, the school's special education budget can be spared the cost of extra academic services. This kind of interference from principals and teachers has become so widespread that some states have enacted laws that expressly forbid teachers from giving parents advice on psychiatric diagnoses and medications.[18]

WHEN TEACHERS ACT AS PSYCHIATRISTS: A CAUTIONARY TALE

I have treated countless children whose teachers inappropriately pressured their parents to have them diagnosed with mental illnesses and medicated. The case of six-year-old Andy is a poignant illustration of why teachers should not try to act as their students' psychiatrists. Andy was brought to me for a second opinion by his mother, who had adopted him when he was six months old. He had been severely neglected while still in the care of his biological mother, who was addicted to cocaine and alcohol. Andy sustained long-term effects of this early abuse, although he would have no conscious memories of that time. The first months of life are critical to the development of a healthy psyche through the process of attachment with the mother or primary caregiver. Five-plus years of parenting by a healthy and caring mom did not enable Andy to form healthy emotional connections, nor could they reverse the effects of those abusive formative months. As a result, Andy was socially awkward, and his poor social skills led to a lot of conflict with peers. He was withdrawn and unaffectionate with his adoptive mother, resisting her attempts to hug him. At school he was obsessed with being first in line, and he rushed through his schoolwork to be the first to turn in his assignments.

Andy's teacher diagnosed him with ADHD and directed his adoptive mother to get Ritalin from the child's pediatrician. The mother went as directed to the doctor and reported what the teacher had said. The pediatrician dutifully wrote out a prescription for Ritalin, a process which took no more than ten minutes, according to Andy's mother. She didn't see much improvement in Andy while he was taking Ritalin, and finally she came to me for a second opinion. After a thorough interview with Andy, I diagnosed him as having reactive attachment disorder and changed his prescription to an antidepressant. Several weeks later his adoptive mother reported back to me. With tears in her eyes, she told me that her son had actually offered her a hug for the first time since she had adopted him! She said that he was a new boy since treatment with the antidepressant began.

Unfortunately, months later Andy's mother gave me some disturbing news. After she had casually mentioned the change of medication to Andy's teacher, the teacher demanded that Andy be taken off the antidepressant and placed back on Ritalin. The boy's mother felt trapped. Not wanting to anger the teacher, and yet not wanting to see her son lose the improvements he had made on the new medication, she became creative. She told the teacher that she would be restarting the Ritalin and that she would appreciate feedback from her as to how her son performed in class that particular day. When that day arrived, believing that Ritalin had been substituted for the antidepressant, the teacher reported to the mother that she had seen a huge improvement in Andy's behavior at school. In fact, Andy had taken the same antidepressant that day, as he had for the previous two months! Andy's mother had lied to the teacher to avoid further reprimands and possible retribution toward Andy. Meanwhile, she continued the treatment that had been so successful for her son. It was a shame that pressure from the teacher had forced this mother to be dishonest, but she felt it was necessary to protect her son's mental health. Because the teacher had tried to be a doctor, the trust and cooperation between the parent and teacher had been shattered. However, in this case the child did not pay the price for the misdiagnosis; thankfully a quick-thinking mother saved this child from harm.

This does not describe all or even most of the educators with whom I have worked. Unfortunately, it does describe some of them.

Most teachers have excellent classroom management skills and would only suggest a psychiatric evaluation when it is appropriate. However, at times even a well-meaning teacher may draw the wrong conclusions about a child's medical needs.[19]

CASE STUDIES OF CHILDREN WHO HAVE BEEN MISDIAGNOSED WITH BIPOLAR DISORDER

I have seen far too many children who had symptoms that were clearly the result of spoiling (ODD), trauma (PTSD), or drug-induced rages, who instead were diagnosed with bipolar disorder. This diagnosis is currently so popular that children who have temper tantrums will likely be diagnosed with bipolar disorder by at least one person at some point in their childhood. The following case studies of children who have been victims of a bipolar misdiagnosis demonstrate the absurdity and danger of this practice.

Ten-year-old Tommy: Bratty, Not Bipolar

In the children's psychiatric emergency clinic where I assess children who have been committed for suicidal threats or acts of assault, I met a child who exemplified how easily bratty children are diagnosed with bipolar disorder. This ten-year-old boy, who I will call Tommy, had a long history of being medicated with psychotropics for ordinary misbehavior. He had been brought to my unit by the police after he had a temper tantrum at school. Tommy had a reputation for fighting with his peers and defying his teachers that stretched all the way back to kindergarten.

Initially Tommy had been diagnosed with ADHD and was prescribed first Ritalin, then Adderall, followed by Concerta, and finally Strattera. When all of these stimulant medications failed, his diagnosis was ramped up to bipolar disorder, and so were his drugs. He graduated from stimulants to powerful antipsychotics; initially Seroquel and later Risperdal, to which Depakote (an antiseizure medication) was added. The combination of the Risperdal and Depakote caused Tommy to gain 40 extra pounds, a common side effect with either of these two medications. But treatment with antipsychotic drugs didn't stop his belligerence. Each new prescription sedated Tommy slightly, rendering him a little less disruptive at school, but only briefly. After a period of time, he became accustomed to the sedation, and his old bratty behaviors would shine through. Tommy was also provided psychotherapy, both at school and privately, but counseling Tommy didn't change his behavior either.

Tommy's mother was convinced that her son was bipolar and that his behaviors were completely beyond her control. Her parenting approach consisted of pleading or threatening. When he escalated his tantrums to include hitting her and destroying property in the house, she ultimately conceded to his demands. She was afraid of him, and he knew it. Her parenting style was not only completely ineffective but also detrimental because it was the direct cause of his worsening manipulative angry outbursts. Over the course of years of psychiatric assessments and interventions, his mother was never encouraged or directed to change her parenting approach, and Tommy's behavior didn't improve.

At home Tommy had a bedroom to himself fully outfitted with every creature comfort available to a child. He had a TV, a DVD player, Play Station II, Game Cube, an iPod, a stereo, and a computer with Internet access, which he enjoyed using to converse with others in a chat room. His parents had divorced when Tommy was an infant, so his guilt-ridden mother had attempted to compensate by showering him with treats and toys. Tommy continued to have temper tantrums when he didn't get his way, and he refused to comply with classroom rules and assignments. The school provided him with extensive special education services because every medication trial failed to change his baseline behavior of belligerence and defiance. He was eventually placed in a self-contained classroom for children with poor anger management skills.

Tommy is an excellent example of a child who has slipped through the system unnecessarily medicated because his doctor was either afraid to confront the boy's parents or was clueless. Children like Tommy will continue to be medicated unnecessarily as long as parents are not given the tools to change their parenting style, and as long as there are doctors who collude with parents and teachers by interpreting all negative behaviors as evidence of bipolar illness.

Seventeen-year-old Lori: Cursory Psychiatric Assessment Leads to Misdiagnosis

Seventeen-year-old Lori was hospitalized after a suicide attempt. She was diagnosed with bipolar disorder and put on two medications at the same time—an antidepressant and a mood stabilizer. But Lori's history was completely inconsistent with this diagnosis. She had never had a manic episode and was not even having the anger outbursts that her psychiatrist might have loosely construed as mania to justify his diagnosis. She was experiencing symptoms of depression, anxiety, and nightmares stemming from the rape she had experienced four years earlier. She had flashbacks of the attack, hypervigilance, insomnia, difficulty concentrating, and social withdrawal. Lori was afraid to leave her home. Her rapist was a boy who was attending her high school, and he had never faced any criminal prosecution, prompting Lori to beg her mother to take her out of school to be homeschooled. When I met Lori she reported she had not received any psychiatric care or counseling prior to her psychiatric hospitalization the week before.

Unfortunately, Lori had turned to alcohol and marijuana to escape the emotional pain she carried. The depressant effect of the alcohol, her drug of choice, exacerbated her sad mood. My first step in treating Lori was to help wean her from the drugs and alcohol and encourage her to attend Teen-AA. Then I tapered her off her mood stabilizer (which Lori was convinced was responsible for the side effects she had been experiencing) and increased her dose of antidepressant medication. Lori and I then started regular psychotherapy sessions. Probably her greatest improvement occurred when she stopped drinking alcohol and using marijuana. It was also very beneficial for Lori to have someone in whom she could confide and to be able to unload her emotional burden. I am sure the antidepressants played their part as well.

The most disturbing feature of the psychiatric care Lori received in the hospital was that her psychiatrist jumped to the conclusion that she had bipolar disorder. In making this misdiagnosis he had effectively stopped all of the appropriate treatments that would have really helped her, such as psychotherapy, stopping drinking, and the correct dose of an antidepressant for her actual diagnosis of PTSD.[20]

BIPOLAR TODDLERS AND PRESCHOOLERS

As the following three high-profile cases demonstrate, even children as young as two years old are not immune to being misdiagnosed with bipolar disorder and being prescribed drug cocktails that include potent antipsychotic drugs.

Two-year-old Karen

As reported in the September 2006 issue of *Psychiatric Times*, two-year-old Karen was referred to a clinic that specialized in infant mental health assessments by a physician who was already treating her with an antipsychotic drug for her aggression. Clinic psychiatrist Mary Gleason explained that these types of referrals were all too common at their clinic. Karen's presenting symptoms included aggression, irritability, and oppositional behavior, in the context of escalating abuse by her father directed at both Karen and her mother. During the assessment, Karen's mother revealed that she had projected her fear of and anger toward her husband onto her daughter "She is mean, just like her father," Karen's mother claimed. When Karen and her mother were observed together by the assessment team, it became evident that Karen confounded her mother with mixed signals that spoke to Karen's ambivalent feeling about her mother—approaching her for comfort and then hitting her. Treatment included directing Karen and her mother to safe housing away from her abusive father, discontinuation of the antipsychotic drug, and parent–child psychotherapy. Karen's mother was also treated for the post-traumatic stress disorder caused by her husband's abuse. Over the next few months, Karen's aggression decreased, her sleep improved, and mother and daughter started to show true enjoyment of each other for the first time.[21] Karen's case illustrates how doctors rush to medicate children—even as young as two years old—instead of conducting a thorough evaluation that puts the child's belligerent behaviors in context.

Three-year-old Matthew

As reported by Stephanie Hockridge on the CBS News in February 2007, three-year-old Matthew was referred to a psychiatrist by his school district because of his aggressive, impulsive, and risk-taking behavior. The psychiatrist diagnosed him with bipolar disorder and prescribed the antipsychotic Risperdal for him. When his mother Carolyn tried to get the prescription filled, five different pharmacists refused to fill it. The prescribing doctor finally convinced a pharmacist to fill the prescription, but by this point Carolyn and her husband realized how powerful and dangerous the drug must be. "I would get up at all times of the night and go over there to make sure he was still breathing. I hurt, my heart hurt. I cried just about every night before I'd go to bed," Carolyn said. But despite all the effort and risk involved in giving Matthew Risperdal, the drug not only failed to address any of his symptoms, it actually enhanced his aggression. Matthew's parents then took him to a different doctor, who diagnosed the boy's condition as ADHD and prescribed Ritalin. But this drug made him nauseous. Next the doctor tried Clonidine, an antihypertensive drug that is increasingly used "off label" to treat ADHD. But Clonidine induced terrifying hallucinations that caused Matthew to wake up screaming in the middle of the night. This was the last straw for Carolyn; she took Matthew off all of his medications.

Then the phone calls from the school began again. Teachers and administrators were complaining that Matthew just wasn't behaving. A trip to a third doctor rendered a new diagnosis—depression—which came with yet another prescription. At this point Matthew's father put his foot down and insisted that they find someone who could help their son without using drugs. Matthew's parents finally consulted with psychologist David Stein, who recognized that ineffectual and inconsistent parental discipline was the primary source of Matthew's out-of-control behavior. He counseled Matthew's parents about how to provide Matthew with structured and consistent discipline, and after a short time, his extreme behavior subsided.

"It's a night-and-day difference," explained Matthew's father. "He's a totally different child, he's happy, he tells you that he loves you at any old time," added his mother. [22]

Four-year-old Rebecca

At two years of age, Rebecca Riley was diagnosed with both ADHD and bipolar disorder by her psychiatrist Kayoko Kifuji of the Tufts-New England Medical Center. Two years later, on December 13, 2006, four-year-old Rebecca died as a result of a lethal combination of the medications prescribed by Dr. Kifuji: Depakote (an antiseizure medication), Seroquel (an antipsychotic), and Clonidine (an antihypertensive drug).

To provide a context for understanding how this child's health care had been mismanaged, some family background is needed. Just prior to Rebecca's death, her father, Michael Riley, had been charged with attempted rape, sexual assault, and giving pornography to Rebecca's thirteen-year-old sister. Mr. Riley had been ordered by the court not to enter the home where Rebecca and her family were living until a pending investigation had been completed. He had been freed on $25,000 bail, posted by Rebecca's mother Carolyn. The thirteen-year-old sister was still in protective custody with the state social services department.

The parents had originally taken Rebecca to see the psychiatrist in an attempt to have their two-year-old daughter diagnosed with bipolar disorder so she could receive Social Security Disability Insurance (SSDI) benefits like the rest of the children. Rebecca's two siblings (ages eleven and six) and her father had all been diagnosed with bipolar disorder and had been awarded SSDI benefits for this disability. Carolyn Riley, Rebecca's mother, had also been awarded a social security benefit check for her mental illness; depression, and anxiety. At the time of Rebecca's death, both parents were unemployed, collected a welfare check along with their SSDI benefit checks, and lived in subsidized housing.

It is essential to understand that without Dr. Kifuji's cooperation the family could never have qualified for their SSDI benefit checks.

The Social Security Administration would have required a written report prepared by a doctor to verify that each applicant had a legitimate diagnosis that rendered him or her completely disabled in order for each member of the Riley family to receive a benefit check. Indeed, Dr. Kifuji would have had to submit a written report for each of the Riley children, including Rebecca. Over the years, all three children had been taken to the same psychiatrist, Dr. Kifuji, and each one was diagnosed with bipolar disorder and ADHD. Their mother was seeking social security benefits for all three children, but at the time of Rebecca's death, she had only succeeded in getting SSDI benefits for the older two. This raises the issue of the parents' motives in taking a two-year-old child to a psychiatrist in the first place.

In violation of the restraining order against him, Michael Riley was in the home on the night of Rebecca's death. He was directing Carolyn Riley to increase the dosage of the Clonidine, which ultimately killed Rebecca, because he wanted to quiet her down. As Michael Riley stated to the police, they were trying to silence her incessant coughing because "It was getting really annoying, that she was keeping everybody awake." Despite the pleading of Rebecca's uncle, James McGonnell, to take the child to the hospital, the parents continued to medicate her further through the night.

McGonnell and his girlfriend Kelly Williams, who lived with the Rileys, told police that the Rileys would put their kids to bed as early as 5:00 PM. Rebecca, they said, often slept through the day and got up only to eat. McGonnell and Williams told police that when Rebecca's father decided the kids were "acting up," he would tell Carolyn to give them more pills. According to McGonnell and Williams, Rebecca spent the last days of her life wandering around the house, sick and disoriented. But the Rileys told police that they were not alarmed. "It was just a cold," Carolyn repeatedly said during police interviews. Prosecutors say the Rileys intentionally tried to quiet their daughter with high doses of Clonidine. Relatives told police the Rileys called Clonidine the "happy medicine" and the "sleep medicine."

Williams told police that the night before Rebecca died, she was pale and seemed "out of it." At one point, Williams said, the little girl knocked weakly on her parents' bedroom door and softly called for her mommy, but Michael Riley opened the door a crack and yelled at her to go back to her room. Later that night, McGonnell told police, he heard someone struggling to breathe and found Rebecca gurgling as if something were stuck in her throat. McGonnell told police he wiped vomit from his niece's face, and then kicked in the door to her parents' room and yelled at them to take Rebecca to the emergency room. Instead, Carolyn Riley said, she gave her daughter another half-tablet of Clonidine.[23]

The parents told the police they were only following the doctor's orders regarding the amounts and types of medication they gave their child on the night she died of a drug overdose. Dr. Kifuji maintained she had done nothing wrong in spite of the fact that she had simultaneously prescribed Depakote, Seroquel, and Clonidine for Rebecca when she was only two years old. The autopsy revealed that at the time of her death, Rebecca had all three psychiatric medications and two cold remedies (dextromethorphan, a cough suppressant, and chlorpheniramine, an antihistamine) in her system. In spite of her claim of innocence, Dr. Kifuji has agreed to stop practicing medicine until the conclusion of the state medical board's investigation of her treatment of Rebecca.[24]

Rebecca's death has inflamed a long-running debate in psychiatry. Some psychiatrists believe that bipolar disorder, which was traditionally diagnosed only in adolescence or early adulthood, has become a trendy diagnosis in young children. "As a clinician, I can tell you it's just very difficult to say whether someone is just throwing tantrums or has bipolar disorder," said Dr. Oscar G. Bukstein, a child psychiatrist and associate professor at the University of Pittsburgh.[25]

How can there be any doubt in the minds of thinking individuals that Rebecca was inappropriately medicated with psychiatric drugs? If Dr. Kifuji had been more concerned with the health and welfare of this little girl, Rebecca might be alive today. Did Dr. Kifuji inquire about Rebecca's home life? About the whereabouts of the child-molesting father? About the adjustment the small child was making to her thirteen-year-old sister's placement outside their home? If Dr. Kifuji had made the effort to understand the life of her four-year-old patient, she might have understood why this little girl was angry and upset. Instead, the doctor accepted the mother's description of Rebecca's behavior and assumed there had to be a neurotransmitter deficiency that required medicating. The same attitude of arrogance on the part of many psychiatrists has led to an explosive rise in the inappropriate medicating of young minds.

In the children's psychiatric emergency clinic where I consult, I have seen a multitude of cases where parents are seeking social security disability benefits for their children based on a mental illness. In one case, a mother who completely indulged her three-year-old son was frustrated that he would not behave for her. The boy's father reported that he never had any disciplinary problems with his son. The mother pressed on, oblivious to the father's testimony, and reported to me that she herself had diagnosed her son with bipolar disorder, which, she informed me, entitled her to social security disability benefits and medications to quiet the boy.

A woman once came to the crisis clinic with her eighteen-month-old child, making the very same case for medications and requesting a benefit check based on her own research and conclusion that her child had bipolar disorder. Another mother was so blatantly fixed on getting me to endorse her claim for her child's social security benefit that she actually told her five-year-old daughter to "act up for the doctor so we can get a check." It has become increasingly common in the practice of child psychiatry to encounter patients whose parents are seeking SSDI benefits for their children based on a psychiatric diagnosis. This adds one more layer of complications for a responsible child psychiatrist to sort through when evaluating a child with behavior problems.

WHERE DO WE GO FROM HERE? A MESSAGE TO PARENTS

When a normal but bratty child is misdiagnosed with bipolar disorder, almost everyone benefits. The school gets more funding, the teacher has a more subdued student in his already busy classroom, and the parents may benefit financially and be relieved of responsibility or blame for their child's disruptive behavior. Everyone benefits— except for the child, who is burdened by the label of mental illness, prescribed a medication that could endanger his health, and denied the help and support he needs.

Parents must put the needs of their children before their own needs when they seek a psychiatric diagnosis for their misbehaving child. Parents' efforts to avoid an uncomfortable confrontation with their belligerent child may spare them a headache in the short-term, but only at the long-term expense of their child. Guidance and discipline should be provided to a child, and the sooner this happens, the better. The longer parents wait to address their misbehaving youngster, the harder their job will be. Rushing to a psychiatrist for absolution from parental guilt will not correct a child's behavior problems and will put the child at medical risk. Unfortunately, families have no idea what risks they take when stepping into the office of a child psychiatrist to seek medications for their misbehaving children.

A MESSAGE TO CHILD PSYCHIATRISTS

There was a time in the profession of child psychiatry when doctors insisted on hours of evaluation before making a diagnosis or prescribing a medication. Today many of my colleagues in psychiatry make an initial assessment of a child and write a prescription in less than twenty minutes. Parents have reported to me that their pediatrician took only five minutes to assess and medicate. Who's the winner in this race, other than the HMOs? Parents eager to fix their child's problems pressure doctors to provide fast relief with a pill. Unfortunately, most doctors usually reach for the one and only tool they are familiar with: medication. Medicine is what they know best, and it is often what parents expect from the psychiatrist.

Doctors under the pressure of practicing in the managed care environment will spend less and less time with each patient and rush to a quick diagnosis with little, if any, explanation to the family regarding the risks of the psychiatric drugs they prescribe. Well-intentioned but hurried doctors carry the greatest responsibility in this complex system that drives the current practice of overmedicating children. Doctors should take the time to understand their pediatric patients better, and have the courage to deliver the bad news that sometimes a child's disruptive, aggressive, and defiant behavior is caused by poor parenting, not a chemical imbalance.

I cannot stress enough the importance of a careful, honest, and thorough evaluation prior to medicating a child. Psychiatrists must have the courage to withstand the pressures placed on them by guilt ridden parents or frazzled teachers. Doctors must put the welfare and safety of their pediatric patients ahead of the push by their managed care contract to get assessments done quickly. Every possible psychotherapeutic intervention should be explored and implemented before a doctor reaches for her prescription pad. If a child must be prescribed medications, it is crucial to proceed with caution. Correctly prescribed for a legitimate mental illness, a psychiatric medication can enable a child to function more normally, and can even save his life. Casually prescribed, a psychiatric medication can destroy his life.[26]

6

Disrupted Care and Disruptive Moods: Pediatric Bipolar Disorder in Foster-Care Children

Toni Vaughn Heineman

There is broad consensus within the mental health community that bipolar disorder (BD) is a serious, genetically influenced mental illness with well-defined diagnostic criteria for older adolescents and adults. When left untreated, adult-onset bipolar disorder can devastate the lives of afflicted individuals and their families. The depressive episodes that are characteristic of BD carry a high risk of suicide, and the grandiosity and loss of reality testing that accompanies full-blown manic states can lead to dangerous behaviors that threaten lives and livelihoods.

By contrast, confusion and disagreements abound among mental health professionals, pediatricians, and parents about when or even whether to diagnose troubled or troubling children with bipolar disorder. Until recently, childhood-onset bipolar disorder was considered rare. Also the diagnostic criteria currently in use for pediatric BD differ so significantly from those used for adult BD that it is not at all clear that the majority of children so labeled are suffering from the same illness as their adult counterparts. Although adults diagnosed with BD typically experience distinct episodes of depression and mania of at least one week in duration, the emotional shifts that have become identified with pediatric BD can include moods that shift within the span of minutes rather than weeks. Some researchers and practitioners would argue that rapid-cycling BD in children is consistent with children's generally greater susceptibility to fluctuations in mood. However, broad diagnostic criteria run the risk of labeling with

BD those children who are healthy but emotionally intense, as well as those whose emotional development has been derailed through chronic neglect or abuse.

EMOTIONAL DEVELOPMENT AND QUALITY OF CARE

Emotions are not simple instincts that emerge full blown at birth. Children do not enter the world with a mature capacity to experience, express, recognize, and regulate their feelings. Rather emotional development unfolds over time and depends on the quality and stability of relationships with parents and other caregivers. Therefore, even mentally healthy children are more reactive to their bodily states, thoughts, and experiences than adults; and they are less able to understand what causes them to feel the way they do or, at times, to even recognize and name the emotions that they're experiencing. For example, an adult can understand that working long hours for several days to meet an important deadline is the cause of her simultaneous feelings of exhaustion, euphoria, relief, and hyperarousal, whereas a ten- or twelve-year-old who has worked intensively to complete a school project may not easily recognize that her unsettled, distractible, excited, and tired feelings are to be expected under the circumstances. When assessing a child's emotional well-being, it is of critical importance to be knowledgeable about what is expectable and acceptable at a particular stage of development.

Parents' appropriate and predictable responses to their children's moods, behaviors, and body language build and strengthen the neurological foundation for self-regulation and emotional maturity. For example, most parents learn to recognize and respond swiftly to the cry that signals their baby's hunger. Intuitively a parent may also name the unsettling feeling and its solution: "Oh, you are so hungry. There, there. Let's get the bottle to fill up your hungry tummy." Over time, the child learns to identify this physical sensation—a particular uncomfortable feeling in the belly—as hunger and to know that the discomfort can be relieved with food. If we fast-forward fifteen years into the future, we can imagine this child, now a teenager, striding into the kitchen and announcing to his mother, "I'm starving. How long until dinner? What's to eat—right now?"

But what if his mother was depressed and too self-absorbed to learn to discriminate among his different cries so that she sometimes responded to a hunger cry with a bottle, at other times with a diaper change, and at other times not at all. Perhaps her words and tone of voice mislabeled both the problem and its solution: "You are so demanding. You just need to cry it out and learn to leave me alone."

Over time, her child will become increasingly oblivious to or confused by his feelings. Without the attention of an attuned caregiver, children continue to have the global physiological responses of early infancy rather than the nuanced states that gradually develop over the course of childhood and adolescence. Under these circumstances children do not actually experience more discrete feeling states, let alone learn how to name them. Without the experience of a range of feeling states, a child has no reliable way of signaling his needs and has even less sense of the kinds of responses that might diminish his distress and increase his pleasure. Under these circumstances we can imagine him as an adolescent who barges into the kitchen, unhappy and uncomfortable, but unaware that he is hungry. He might reject an offer of food with, "It's not that easy. Leave me alone. I'll take care of myself."

Relationships beget relationships, and children who have been mistreated are prone to mistreating others. A child or teenager who has been subjected to years of neglect or abuse is likely to have a limited capacity for empathy because she has not learned to differentiate, identify, or name her own or other people's feelings. She may also disregard or vigorously reject offers of help or support when she feels unhappy or uncomfortable. From the perspective of a child whose early needs were routinely ignored, misinterpreted, or discounted, it makes no sense to take later offers of help seriously. Gestures of care can also threaten her sense of emotional safety. A child who has had to learn self-reliance at a tender age does not easily risk making herself vulnerable by placing her trust in yet another person, who might once again break her heart. Instead she may appear needy and dependent one moment and then reject an offer of comfort with an attitude of fierce independence the next. This kind of seeming emotional lability in children with a history of trauma is likely to reflect both a developmental deficit arising from impoverished experience and a defensive strategy to cope with that deficit.

ASSESSING EMOTIONALLY DISTURBED CHILDREN

As illustrated above, bipolar disorder is only one of many potential causes for emotional turbulence in childhood and adolescence, one that locates the difficulty in the child's genetic makeup. As debate about when to diagnose pediatric bipolar disorder and how to treat it continues, mental health professionals would be hard-pressed to disagree with the following bedrock guidelines:

1. Accurate diagnosis requires a detailed assessment that takes into account the child's personal history in order to consider all precipitating

factors and to determine whether there is any familial genetic loading for mood disorders.

2. After a diagnosis is rendered, treatment must be carefully planned and individually tailored, and the child must be closely monitored and have access to continuity of care.

With few exceptions however, research and clinical reports on children diagnosed with bipolar disorder do not take environmental influences such as quality and stability of parenting into account. For children in the foster-care system, information that might lead to a different diagnosis—reactive attachment disorder or complex post-traumatic stress disorder, for example—is simply not available. Vulnerable children, such as those who live in poverty, have been subjected to familial or community violence, or have endured multiple losses in the foster-care system, are at even greater risk for receiving a psychiatric label, unfortunately often after a cursory assessment and a hastily conceived plan of treatment with little opportunity for continuity of care.

THE RISE OF PEDIATRIC BIPOLAR DISORDER AMONG CHILDREN IN FOSTER CARE

I have worked with children in the foster-care system for nearly thirty years. At the beginning of my career, medicating children with the few psychoactive drugs available was done with great caution. In the intervening years, the armamentarium of medications available to increase attention, stabilize moods, quiet hallucinations, induce sleep, ease depression, and calm anxiety has swelled almost beyond belief. Coincidentally, during the same time period the rolls of the foster-care system also swelled and are just now beginning to drop as the children who came into care as a result of the crack epidemic are reaching adulthood and leaving the system. For foster children the diagnosis of bipolar disorder is particularly problematic—for many it connotes "craziness" in a way that anxiety or depression do not. They can more easily relate to the idea that they are depressed because they have lost their family or friends or community, or are anxious because they don't know where they might live next week. "Anxious" and "depressed" are used in the general population to describe a wide range of moods. However, "bipolar disorder" is purely a psychiatric diagnosis that locates the problem in the child, rather than taking into account the possibility that periods of intense anxiety juxtaposed with periods of intense depression might also be a response to an unpredictable and bleak environment. The young adults now leaving the foster-care system are more likely to suffer psychiatric disturbance, including mood disorders, than their peers. Perhaps they entered the system with a genetic loading from parents who are unavailable to provide a history. They have also been exposed to more trauma than their peers. In those instances when we have at least cursory information about a traumatic history and no information about family history, we must not favor a genetic basis of behavior over environmental influences when most likely a complex set of interactions between nature and nurture is at work.

Children enter foster care from a position of vulnerability. Many of them are born to low-income mothers who have had little or no prenatal care. Many have been exposed to significant amounts of alcohol and illicit drugs in utero. Some go directly from the hospital's newborn nursery to a foster home. Others live for several weeks, months, or years with parents and extended family members who, because of poverty, mental illness, addiction, incarceration, or a background of abuse and neglect, are ill prepared to raise children, particularly those who enter the world with a compromised neurological system. Children who enter foster care when they are older have frequently suffered from neglect. Some have been physically or sexually abused; many have witnessed domestic violence, and many more have been exposed to community violence.

Simply put, stability and predictability in the form of loving and reliable care has been notably lacking in the lives of children entering foster care whether they enter as infants, toddlers, children, or adolescents. As a result it is frequently the case that their emotional development has been stunted and they have a limited ability to recognize or regulate their emotions. Instead they remain reliant on others to recognize that hunger requires food, that agitation requires calming, that sadness requires soothing, or that fear requires confident protection. Indeed they often have difficulty distinguishing between their internal and external worlds. With limited capacity for self-soothing, they are neurologically primed for heightened responsiveness.

When we place a child who is emotionally unstable and unpredictable into a system that is itself unstable and unpredictable, it is hardly surprising that it is difficult to know, from one minute to the next, how the child may feel or behave. And so it is not unusual for foster children to display both more intense moods and more frequent and rapid shifts in mood and behavior than we would expect from children of similar ages and developmental stages. In the current climate, in which bipolar disorder has become such a popular diagnosis, we can see how easily foster children might be suspected of having this disorder, and how important it is to first rule out other ways of understanding their chaotic emotions.

ANGIE: A CASE STUDY

"Angie," a young teenager in foster care, was diagnosed with bipolar disorder. Her brush with the mental health system illustrates how difficult it is for children in foster care to receive an assessment and follow-up care that meet even the minimal standards described earlier. Angie's story may invoke intense feelings—sadness and despair along with annoyance and rage—feelings that we associate with pediatric bipolar disorder and also with a sense of overwhelming helplessness in the face of unbearable circumstances.

Angie, a fifteen-year-old living in a group home was taken to a hospital emergency room because she had been crying uncontrollably for ten days. She had been spending most of each day in bed and showed little interest in activities, school, or meals. At times she was unresponsive, seeming not to see or hear when people tried to communicate with her. During the intake interview at the hospital, Angie rocked in her chair with her arms wrapped tightly over her chest. Occasionally her sobs and swaying were interrupted with quiet moans as her hands pulled at her hair. She could barely answer the interviewer's questions and seemed not to understand or be able to explain her unhappiness. After a cursory interview the emergency room psychiatrist gave her a diagnosis of major depression, prescribed an antidepressant, and recommended that Angie return to the outpatient psychiatry clinic for follow-up care. This diagnosis was now a part of Angie's medical and social service record.

The piece of the story that did not make it into the hospital record was the fact that Angie's boyfriend, also a foster child, had been suddenly moved to a group home out of the area when his foster mother had become ill and unable to care for him. He and Angie were too young to drive, and there was no reliable public transportation to connect their two communities. This unexpected loss was predictably heart-wrenching for Angie, who was fully in the sway of her first love. They had not even had a chance to say good-bye to each other.

Angie had been in her current group home for a very short time when this abrupt separation occurred, and to make matters worse, the only staff member whom she had felt close to had recently left. Angie was bereft; the only two people in the world to whom she felt connected were gone. There was no one to comfort her, to help her think creatively about how she might reconnect with her boyfriend, or to advocate for her being able to see him. Angie could only hold and rock herself like the infant she felt herself to be. She became inarticulate, unable to express her overwhelming grief in words; and no one was available to hear her words, even if she could have found them. In her regressed state, her only forms of communication were moans and sobs. She had no reliable caregiver to help her name her feelings and connect them with the events that had devastated and depleted her emotional resources. Angie desperately needed someone who could not only offer physical comfort in the moment, but also help her to interpret and cope with her feelings so they would not overwhelm her. She needed someone who could hold out hope of a brighter future for her—someone who could know that her emotions, overwhelming as they were, would gradually dissipate and become manageable so that she could reclaim the emotional resources she needed to function.

Lacking the care she desperately needed at this crucial time, the stage was set for an emotional breakdown. Angie began to emerge from her depression after about two weeks, and she did so with a vengeance. She angrily refused her boyfriend's phone calls, insisting that she hadn't really cared about him and didn't miss him at all. In like fashion, Angie rebuffed the efforts of staff in the group home to reengage her in activities she had previously seemed to enjoy. Instead she filled her time by frantically and compulsively text-messaging everyone on her contact list. Her school performance declined as a result of frequent absences that, more often than not, involved sexual encounters with boys older and rougher than she had formerly associated with. When she did attend school her teachers noted that she was disheveled and seemed to be particularly distracted and disorganized. The staff at the group home became increasingly irritated with Angie, and she with them. It seemed that whenever there was a verbal or physical altercation in the home, Angie was at its center. After two weeks the owner of the home, who had a reputation for "running a very tight ship," initiated Angie's removal. Angie's behavior in the next group home continued to escalate, and after two weeks she was placed in a short-term residential treatment facility. Based on the earlier diagnosis of a major depressive episode and on her recent behavior, Angie's admitting diagnosis was early-onset bipolar disorder.

Experts agree that a diagnosis of bipolar disorder cannot be made definitively without a thorough assessment. But conducting an adequate assessment hinges on a series of unarticulated assumptions that (1) the child will be consistently available to participate; (2) qualified mental health specialists will conduct the assessment; (3) the evaluator will have access to adults who know the child; and (4) there will be sufficient funds available to pay for the assessment. These assumptions ignore the reality that, more often than not, hospitals, clinics, and individuals working with foster youth face insurmountable challenges in finding the time, money, and information necessary for a careful and thorough assessment. Although government funding may be available, the rate of reimbursement is typically so low that clinicians in private practice often refuse to see foster children or strictly limit the number of hours they make available to them. As a result, the pool of experienced child psychiatrists and psychologists available to this population in the private sector is very small. Foster youth referred to a hospital or clinic for evaluation and treatment sometimes have access to more resources. However, as we will see, other factors frequently interfere.

Angie's placement in a residential treatment setting took her to a community more than one hundred miles from the city of her birth and childhood. Because of her changed status, she was assigned a new caseworker. The transfer of her most recent file from her former caseworker to her new one took nearly a week. The transfer of those records to the residential treatment center took another week; and retrieving two other folders, which contained the remainder of her records from storage, consumed an additional two weeks. By the time those records arrived, Angie had been discharged. The staff had diagnosed and treated her without having any significant information about her history. Angie was able to give them some information, but her willingness to engage with the staff varied significantly, as did her moods. She was sometimes depressed and tearful and sometimes angry, sullen, and stubbornly silent. The information she did offer was sketchy and sometimes confused, but reality based.

When the file finally arrived at the treatment center, it confirmed Angie's report that she had been in foster care since the age of five. Prior to that, she had lived for some period—possibly a year or two—with maternal relatives. She had apparently moved from household to household, depending on which relative had the space, time, and energy to care for a small child. The recorded information about her early life was limited. Her parents had grown up in the same neighborhood. Shortly after Angie's birth her father was killed in a gang-related drive-by shooting, although it is not clear whether he was the shooter's target or an uninvolved bystander. Angie presumably had little or no contact with her paternal relatives.

Her mother was sixteen when Angie was born, and was in and out of Angie's life for the first few years. By the time Angie entered foster care, her relatives did not even know how to reach the mother. They believed she supported herself largely through prostitution, and reported that she would show up periodically, wanting to see Angie and demanding money. Angie's maternal grandmother suspected that Angie had witnessed her mother engaging in sex on many occasions.

Angie began her tenure in the foster-care system as a sad, quiet little girl. During her first six months, she was in two different emergency placements followed by three years in a long-term foster placement with an elderly woman who typically cared for four or five foster children at any time. When her foster mother died, Angie became even more quiet and withdrawn. Members of the extended family of her foster-care mother expressed interest in adopting Angie, and at the very least wished to stay in touch with her. For reasons not made clear in the file, the adoption didn't materialize. With the move to a new foster home she lost her friends in her old neighborhood. Her grades in her new school declined, and she was described as a child who was distant, kept to herself, and didn't make friends easily.

Over the next four years Angie was in three more foster homes. One foster mother moved to another state in order to be with her children. Another asked that Angie and her other charges be sent to respite care for two weeks during her vacation, but if the woman did return from her travels, she didn't notify anyone. The respite-care family did not want to become long-term foster parents, necessitating Angie's move to yet another home. While she was in that home, another foster child accused the foster parents' biological son of molesting her, and all of the children were removed. Angie, who was then twelve, was moved to the first of two group homes and from there to residential treatment.

Angie was discharged from the residential treatment center before an evaluation was completed because she was not considered a danger to herself or others and she exhibited no psychotic ideation. Her caseworker could not make a case for extending her stay at the center and felt that her treatment could be adequately continued at an outpatient clinic in her own community. Angie returned "home" but went into a different group home placement. The diagnosis that had begun as major depression, based on her visit to the emergency room, and then transformed into bipolar disorder on the basis of descriptions of her behavior by staff members who barely knew her, was now "official"—not as the result of a careful and thorough assessment, but because, very simply, it just got passed along. Unfortunately, Angie's story is all too familiar in the foster-care system. There are simply not enough people with enough time, information, or funding to adequately assess and properly treat these vulnerable young people.

Based on the limited information about her mother's lifestyle, it is possible that she exposed Angie to street drugs in utero, potentially compromising her neurological development and making her vulnerable to psychiatric disturbance. Angie's primary responses to the repeated losses in her early life were depression and withdrawal, and her depressed, angry reactions to her boyfriend's departure were intense. Perhaps her response was indicative of a genetic loading for mood disorders, but without access to her family history, this supposition remains speculative. We *do* know, however, that the chaotic and disrupted care that Angie received throughout her childhood posed significant risks to her emotional development, so that Angie's responses to her circumstances may have been simply those of a child who has lost too many loved ones without the support to manage the attendant feelings. Young love is particularly intense—whether the love of a baby or toddler for her parent, or the first romantic love of early adolescence. The sudden and unexpected loss of her first boyfriend may have triggered in Angie memories and repressed feelings of grief and loss from her earliest years. If Angie had had a loving parent or caregiver to support her and to know, when she couldn't, that the pain of her loss would diminish, she might gradually have been able to cope with the rush of confusing emotions she was experiencing. If someone—anyone—had understood how important this relationship was and had helped Angie find and contact her lost love, things might have been different for her.

If the emergency room psychiatrist had known about Angie's loss, would the diagnosis have been different? Psychiatrists receive much more training in the diagnosis and management of biochemically-based mental illnesses than in understanding suffering that stems from the losses, disappointments, setbacks, and disillusionments of life. Compounding the tendency to diagnose what can be medically treated is the reality that funding for treatment hinges on a medical diagnosis. Paradoxically, clinicians sometimes give foster children a diagnosis that may not be entirely accurate—such as depression, obsessive-compulsive disorder, or bipolar disorder—in the belief that the diagnosis will ensure treatment. Although this may be true, the treatment that follows an incorrect diagnosis often does more harm than good. Foster children commonly report that they were either given medication when they just wanted to talk to someone, or were denied mental health services because their problems weren't "bad enough." Of course, some of these children do benefit from a medical intervention, and their descriptions of their encounters with mental health professionals are subject to distortion, but these negative reports occur with such frequency that we cannot reasonably ignore them.

If we now revisit the minimal criteria for accurately diagnosing and treating early-onset bipolar disorder—a careful and extensive evaluation that establishes a genetic predisposition and a clear and well-coordinated treatment plan—we see that Angie's experience falls significantly short. Although the staff at the residential treatment center had consistent contact with Angie for two weeks prior to her diagnosis, they had no history—no baseline against which to view her moods and behavior. The information in her file, when it finally arrived, provided a patchwork history because it had been compiled by a series of caseworkers based on very limited personal contact with Angie, her biological relatives, and a series of foster parents.

A typical emergency room visit does not allow any clinician, regardless of training or experience, sufficient time to make a definitive psychiatric diagnosis. This is particularly true for a diagnosis of bipolar disorder, which requires a knowledge of family history. Arriving at an accurate diagnosis is all the more challenging when the person in distress is a young, virtually speechless adolescent like Angie. The reports of group home staff members provided the basis for the next stage of the diagnostic process—depression was transformed into manic depression. When Angie moved from residential treatment to yet another group home, there was no treatment plan, only a supply of medication.

And so we see the inordinate difficulties in trying to construct, coordinate, and monitor a treatment plan for children in the foster-care system. It is entirely unclear who in this cast of characters should have had responsibility for formulating a plan for Angie's treatment, which adults would be involved in its execution, and who would monitor its effectiveness. Although there were many adults in Angie's life, none of them knew her—who she was or where she came from. There was no one to keep Angie in mind—to hold for her a past and a future so that she could live in the present. The loss of a coherent narrative—a cohesive picture of one's life—is perhaps the most enormous and insidious loss for foster children.

Bipolar disorder is an illness that causes great suffering; we trivialize the experiences of those who struggle to overcome its terrible power by carelessly confusing it with other disorders. As we move forward in our efforts to describe, define, and accurately diagnose early-onset BD, it is imperative that we strive to conduct a thorough assessment for each child with a detailed personal history and description of current conditions, in addition to gathering information about genetic and behavioral history.

Alumni of the foster-care system are diagnosed with a wide range of mental illnesses including bipolar disorder at a significantly higher rate than their peers. And so we must pay particular attention to this vulnerable group of children, adolescents, and young adults and must develop better resources for early detection and accurate diagnosis. At the same time, we must carefully consider the possibility that in many instances, it is the system, rather than the child, that is the carrier of the disorder. Foster children often grow up with no sense of their own history in a system that frequently fails to provide them consistent access to responsible caregivers. Children simply cannot develop the capacity for emotional stability in an unstable system. We must not further traumatize children who grow up in foster care by callously ignoring the impact of the external world on their internal lives.

7

Pediatric Bipolar Disorder and the Destruction of Lived Experience: A Case Study

William J. Purcell

What is the fate of our children's lived experience, within a mental health system that emphasizes psychopharmacological treatment and brief interventions? By lived experience I mean nothing more or less than children's memory and understanding of their lives, including their attachments, losses, aspirations, longings, and fears.

We all expect to draw meaning from our lived experience. Most of us wish to create our lives and ourselves from what we feel and think and from what we have lived. Our notion of truth derives in part from the opportunity to reflect on our lives honestly and fairly, and to discover what is authentic or real in ourselves, even if that reality is inconvenient and unpleasant to ourselves or to others. And so it is of utmost importance to consider how our children's lived experience is acknowledged or not acknowledged, valued or dismissed, within the psychiatric system of care.

In recent years we have witnessed an acceleration of broad social trends whose net effect has been to dislocate and destabilize family life. These include increases in single-parent families, a significantly higher percentage of children being raised in poverty or near poverty, increasingly turbulent inner cities and impoverished rural areas, a steep rise in children's exposure to violence in their communities and through the media, and less recreational and leisure time for working parents.[1]

The lives of children raised under these conditions are not what we would wish them to be. Not surprisingly, they often struggle creatively with issues of loss and self-worth. In the parlance of a mental health system dominated by the medical model, children are said to have "symptoms" of a psychiatric illness. But are they symptoms of disease or of creative struggle? Our lexicon suggests that core human values are at stake in how we understand these behaviors and how we respond to them.

DOMINIC: A CASE STUDY OF A "BIPOLAR" CHILD

The following case of a child who was diagnosed with bipolar disorder became known to me through my consultation with a large state agency charged with the management of wraparound psychiatric services for children with significant mental illness. Names and incidental biographical information have been changed to protect confidentiality.

This case highlights the striking contrast between biological and humanistic models of treatment, but it is by no means atypical in its presentation of treatment approaches and diagnostic decision making as they exist in programs such as this. Most importantly, the individual case study is best suited to present the lived experience of children and families as they engage in treatment.

Dominic was five years old when his father first sought help for him. Dominic was a child of slight build with bright brown eyes and a demeanor that suggested he was younger than his actual age. He was not eating well and had lost weight in recent months. His father, Rick, reported that, although Dominic tended to be timid in public settings, he was irritable and defiant at home and threw uncontrolled tantrums with increasing frequency. At night he had difficulty sleeping, seemed to have bad dreams and nightmares, and cried in his sleep.

Dominic's first mental health intervention was conducted by his pediatrician, who believed that Dominic was showing signs of ADHD or a possible mood disorder. The pediatrician knew almost nothing about Dominic's family history beyond the fact that Dominic had come into Rick's care approximately six months prior, after a court proceeding in which Rick won full custody rights and an order of nonvisitation between Dominic and his mother.

When an initial trial of medication failed to alleviate symptoms, Dominic was referred to an outpatient program of intensive services managed by case reviewers in the state Department of Public Welfare. A psychiatrist led the treatment team, which included bachelor's and master's level mental health clinicians. The goal of this program was to provide brief, highly managed, intensive services to children with significant mental health problems.

According to the program's guidelines, the case reviewers sought evidence of measurable behavioral gains on the part of the child in a time frame of one to four months so that the child could be returned to "less restrictive" and less expensive follow-up care. Given the time frame and demands for "measurable gains," the program relied heavily on medication and cognitive behavioral treatment (CBT) approaches. Reviewers regarded more traditional psychotherapy approaches skeptically and discouraged their use.

The program psychiatrist interviewed Dominic and Rick for fifty minutes and concluded that Dominic was suffering from a mood disorder. He prescribed antidepressant medicine for Dominic and referred Dominic and Rick to the treatment team for CBT to support Rick's management of the child's symptoms. The CBT approach sought to modify Rick's responses to Dominic's tantrums and to teach the child rudimentary ways to manage his anger.

The metaphor of "management" seemed to pervade this treatment approach. The case reviewers in the Department of Public Welfare managed the service utilization of the clinical teams. The clinicians managed their caseloads and taught their clients to manage their symptoms. The operation was driven by data (global assessment scales scored by treating clinicians, length of time in services, etc.) and "evidence-based" interventions that lent themselves to programmatic review and management.

After reports of initial improvement, Rick became discouraged and reported that Dominic seemed to be worsening. Following an especially bad night and morning, Rick called the crisis team, and after a brief consultation Dominic was admitted to a local teaching hospital that specialized in child psychiatry. This hospital was also working under a managed care model and sought to limit intervention to brief acute care with a quick return to the community. The treatment model and research interests coincided—the biology and psychopharmacology of mood disorders.

The hospital staff diagnosed Dominic as having pediatric bipolar disorder, and changed his medication. They discharged him after three days and referred him to the intensive outpatient services program. Again there were reports of brief improvement, followed by discouragement. Nonetheless, Dominic was discharged from the intensive services program, and his clinicians entered into the data field that his global assessment score had improved by 15 points at discharge.

Three months later Dominic returned to treatment. His tantrums were continuing, he had lost weight again, and Rick was visibly angrier with him. Rick worried that his job was at risk because of the time and effort required in managing Dominic's behavior. Rick's anger seemed to suggest that he was fending off a feeling of failure as a parent and that his resentment toward Dominic was deepening.

At this point the treatment team was offered consultation with specialists in child and family therapy. It was noted that at no time during the previous interventions (pediatrician, wraparound outpatient program, inpatient program) had a detailed family history been taken. Interviewing was limited to symptom reports, medical history, the completion of various behavioral checklists, and instruction in and review of the medication and CBT approach. The child and family therapy consultants arranged to see Dominic and Rick. Rick was frustrated with treatment and skeptical of any possibility of improvement, but he agreed to attend the sessions. Unlike the previous interventions, which had moved quickly to an ahistorical model of biological causation and the ongoing "management" of behavior, these sessions were conducted with an explicit interest in the family's history and the possible meanings of Dominic's behavior.

In the first session of this consultation, Dominic was encouraged to think about and present his life by an art therapy technique in which the consulting therapist traced his footsteps on a long roll of paper. Each footstep marked a period of time, one year in Dominic's case. For the first empty footstep, the therapist asked Dominic where he was born. Dominic seemed puzzled and said that he didn't know. The therapist suggested that Dominic ask his father to help with filling this first step. Rick came into the room and listened as Dominic asked, "Where was I born?" Rick answered with the name of a local hospital. The therapist wrote the name of the hospital in the heel of the first footprint. Dominic watched intently.

The therapist next asked where Dominic first lived when he came home from the hospital. Dominic looked to Rick, and Rick named a local suburb. "We lived in an apartment on River Street in C___," Rick said. "And who lived in that apartment?" the therapist asked. Dominic again looked to his father. Rick again answered, "Dominic's mother lived there, and I did, and Dominic did, and Dominic's half-sister lived there as well." Dominic's mother was named Maria, and his half-sister was named Jenna. "Let me write the names in the footprint," the therapist said. Dominic watched as the therapist printed the four names in the footprint: Dominic, Rick, Maria, and Jenna. There had been scant mention of Dominic's half-sister in the records, so the therapist asked Rick about her. Jenna was eight years old when Dominic was born. Her father was a previous boyfriend of Maria's, a man whom Rick had never met. Dominic's mother was approximately ten years older than Rick. The apartment they lived in had been hers for two years prior to Rick's moving in. Rick went directly from living with his mother to living with Maria.

The therapist moved to the second footprint. "This footprint represents when Dominic was a one-year-old," the therapist said. The therapist asked the same questions about Dominic's circumstances, and Dominic again looked to his father for answers. At the age of one, Dominic lived with his mother and half-sister. Rick had separated from Maria and returned to living with his mother. Again Dominic listened intently to his father. He looked at the footprint where the three names were inscribed. Dominic took a marker and began to draw a picture of himself and his mother within the footprint. His drawings were rudimentary stick figures. He seemed to become anxious, looked at his father, and then began to scribble over the entire footprint. The therapist completed the remaining footprints in a similar manner. Dominic lived with Maria and Jenna at two, three, and four years of age, and then at five, there was a change—the footprint contained only Dominic and his father.

Dominic had been deeply engrossed in the entire process. The history suggested that Maria had been his primary caretaker until he was more than four years of age and that Jenna had likely been involved in his caretaking as well. Rick had limited sporadic contact with Dominic for three years; then he began to visit more regularly, and when Dominic was in the latter half of his fifth year, Rick took custody and ended Dominic's contacts with Maria and Jenna. The dramatic nature of this change was well illustrated in the series of footprints. The graphic representation of Dominic's history brought these events into the room. A symbolic act is often needed to bring forth the symbolic function of retelling the past.

In a subsequent interview with Rick, the family history was explored in greater depth. Rick had taken custody of Dominic because Maria had a drug problem and was taking poor care of Dominic. With the financial support of his mother he had retained legal counsel, and in a brief hearing obtained custody and a no-visitation order. He felt that Maria did not deserve visits with Dominic and would only be a bad influence on him.

Rick was relying on assistance from his mother in parenting Dominic, although she had limited involvement in previous treatment approaches. Rick worked part-time in both real estate and car sales and was twenty-six years old. His father had left the family when Rick was two years old and he'd had no subsequent contact with his father and did not know where his father lived. He understood that his father had been irresponsible and alcoholic. His mother often spoke badly about Rick's father, and Rick had no desire to know him now.

He had no siblings. He felt that Dominic was lucky to have a father who cared for him, and felt that Dominic did not really miss his mother, much as Rick did not miss his father.

Rick reported that he saw some of Maria's traits in Dominic. He felt that Dominic was stubborn, much as Maria had been, and that he also had difficult moods, just like Maria's. He readily accepted the idea that Dominic had bipolar disorder and believed it likely that Maria had bipolar disorder as well. He reported that this was suggested to him by someone on the hospital staff.

Rick attributed the breakup of his relationship to Maria to her use of drugs and her irresponsibility as a parent. He had no desire to involve her in Dominic's life unless she made "big changes." At the same time he acknowledged, with no apparent sense of contradiction or dissonance, that he had on several occasions told Dominic that he was going to drop him off at Maria's and never come back for him if he continued to misbehave. The nature of this threat was not lost on Dominic. Rick had frequently described Maria's life to Dominic in the bleakest of terms, adding that Dominic was lucky that Rick had rescued him. Rick also reported that on several occasions Maria had sought to breach the no-visitation order, had sent Dominic cards, and had tried surreptitiously to reach him on the phone. None of these issues had been addressed to any extent in the previous interventions. To some degree this was understandable, given Rick's continuing anger and negative judgment of Maria. It likely had been much easier to reach agreement with him through a biological interpretation of Dominic's behavior than to broach these difficult family issues.

Dominic's second session was conducted without Rick's presence in the playroom. Dominic went immediately to the paper showing his footprints and announced that he wanted to draw. However, once the therapist placed crayons and paper in front of him, Dominic could not decide what he wanted to draw. He began to copy another child's drawing, which hung on the playroom wall.

"It's hard to choose what to draw," the therapist reflected to him.

"I want to draw my foot," Dominic said.

With the therapist's assistance he traced his foot on a piece of art paper.

"This is a house," Dominic said, pointing to the empty outline. He drew a cloud sailing above the footprint and a small sun above the cloud. He drew slanted lines representing rain that fell from the cloud. "It's a rainy day," he said, "and everyone has to stay inside."

He drew a square inside of the shoe. "That's the TV," he said. "There's a soap on." He tried to draw a figure inside the TV set, but became frustrated and scribbled over the square. He tried to draw another figure inside the "house" but became frustrated and scribbled over that figure as well.

"It's hard to draw a boy or a girl," the therapist said.

"That's my mother," Dominic said, and he pushed the paper away and began to walk around the playroom. He touched an airplane and then pushed open the lid of the sand tray and became immediately interested in playing in the sand. He used a shovel to make a road. He set up a number of plastic figures, who were the workers making the road. He put a small plastic house at the other end of the sand tray and said that the workers had to plow the road all the way to the house. When asked who lived in the house, Dominic said, "I forget." Then he whispered in the therapist's ear, "They take drugs there," and he placed a female figure in front of the house, lying face down in the sand.

"We have to get there fast," Dominic had one of the road workers say. He then piled handfuls of sand over this female figure and pounded and packed the sand. "She's dead," Dominic said. The therapist said, "The road workers couldn't make the road fast enough and your mother died." "Yes," Dominic said, "and no one will see her anymore."

The therapist said, "Your mother is dead because she took drugs and now she's buried underneath the sand and we won't see her anymore."

"Look," said Dominic, "here's a boy and girl and they're looking for their mother the witch. But she's not a bad witch. She's a good witch." He had two figures, the boy and girl, walk over the sand where the mother figure was buried. "The boy and the girl sit there and begin to cry, wah, wah, wah. Then the father comes over and says, 'You're both babies; you go to sleep and stop crying.'" Dominic had the father figure kick sand around and hit the boy and girl. "I don't like babies," he said. "I don't want any babies in my house."

In a second interview, Rick acknowledged feeling overwhelmed and angry as a parent and said that he was considering moving in with his mother again and letting her do much of the parenting. He described how his mother urged him to get custody of Dominic and went with him to court every day. "She never liked Maria," Rick said. "She warned me not to live with Maria, and she didn't talk to me until Dominic was born. My mother loves Dominic, but she has no use at all for Maria."

In his third play session, Dominic went immediately to the sand tray. After a few minutes of playing with trucks, he set up the house again and this time put the mother figure at a table behind the house. He built up tall hills around the house until the house was surrounded. "It's like a castle," he said. "It's a secret castle and all the knights and the tigers are buried in the sand. Here come the boy and his sister, and they know a secret way into the castle, but a tiger might get them." Dominic made a small opening in the castle wall, behind the house, near the mother and the table. He made the boy and his sister start to crawl through the hole, but then a tiger leapt out from the sand and the boy and the tiger began to fight. The sister managed to get inside the castle and she filled up the hole so the tiger couldn't get in. The boy cried out for help but the tiger pulled him into the wall and the boy was buried there with the tigers and the knights. "The boy is buried there," the therapist said. "Yes," said Dominic. "He can hear them (the mother and sister) eating." Dominic made smacking sounds with his lips; then he began to giggle and smashed everything in the sand tray, saying, "You are bad babies and you'll stay in that bed all night."

In his next interview Rick described some of his difficulties being a parent. He reported that it was hard being a single guy and that he really didn't understand the behavioral approach that had been suggested to him by the previous treatment team. "They didn't understand that once Dominic loses it, there's nothing you can do to get him quieted." Rick asked whether the therapist thought it was a good idea to move back with his mother. The therapist did not answer, but asked if it would be possible to meet Rick's mother and talk with her. Rick seemed hesitant at first but soon assented. "And there's another thing I'd like to do," the therapist said. "With your permission, I'd like to interview Maria." Rick asked why that was necessary. The therapist explained that Dominic's play, and his history of living with Maria, indicated that he maintained strong memories of both his mother and his sister and that these memories and the feelings associated with them were crucial to Dominic's development. Rick appeared skeptical at first and said that he wanted to speak with his attorney, but ultimately agreed to allow the interview.

Maria responded very positively to the opportunity to talk about Dominic and the family situation. She reported that she had completed an inpatient drug rehabilitation program and that she missed Dominic terribly. She expressed a great deal of anger at Rick for denying her visits. She reported that her daughter Jenna also missed Dominic very much. She acknowledged trying to contact Dominic surreptitiously and sending Dominic cards and letters that she doubted he ever got because of Rick's intervention. Maria talked about Dominic's early life and said that he had always been a fussy eater. She described some of the tricks she'd learned to coax him to eat. She indicated that, although she was extremely angry at Rick and did not trust him, she would be willing to work with him in order to have visits with Dominic. She stated that Rick had taken advantage of her through the courts, that she had minimal representation during the custody hearing, and that she had been in a "bad place" during that time. She stated that losing custody of Dominic had been "a wake-up call" for her and that, while attending AA meetings, she had met other parents who had lost custody of their children.

Rick's mother, Rose, was also interviewed. She stated that she felt she could take care of Dominic but that Rick was reluctant to let this happen. She stated that she had warned Rick "from the beginning" about Maria but that he hadn't listened until "it was too late." She did not feel that Maria should be allowed back into Dominic's life. Her hope was that Dominic would "grow out of" his problems and that he would not have the difficulties with drugs that his mother had.

The diagnostic picture that emerged from these sessions indicated that Dominic had suffered an unresolved break in his primary attachment. Rick's wish that Maria be excised from Dominic's life was unrealistic and damaging. Dominic remained preoccupied with the loss of his mother and sister, long after he'd ceased seeing them. Rick's negative statements about Maria were superficially accepted by Dominic, but at a deeper level, they had likely provoked resistance and anxiety in him. Dominic had apparently always been a somewhat picky eater, and fussy eating had once again become a signal of his unhappiness. Dominic's past—that is to say, his primary attachments to Maria and Jenna—remained present in his life, increasingly through negative symptoms and in stark resistance to Rick's exclusion of them. Unwittingly, both Rick and his mother had intensified Dominic's feelings by their repeated negative statements concerning Maria.

Following these evaluation sessions, the consulting therapists suggested the following treatment plan: (1) that Dominic be engaged in individual play therapy in order to express and integrate his feelings about the family situation and the loss of his mother and half-sister; (2) that Rick be engaged in supportive parent counseling designed to assist in deepening his understanding of his son's difficulties with loss and loyalty binds; and (3) that Rick work with the treatment team and Maria to establish visitation among Dominic, Maria, and Jenna. The treatment team indicated that they would not become involved in any possible future custody disputes between the parents but that they would always seek to preserve Dominic's relationship with both parents.

This plan was based on the principles of restoring and strengthening Dominic's primary attachments, and it presumed that his dysregulation was a correlative of the conflict and dysregulation in his family.

The treatment team judged that Dominic was suffering acutely from the loss of his mother and half-sister and that Rick's denial of this issue only exacerbated the difficulty. The treatment plan was presented to Rick in a meeting that his attorney attended. After much discussion and consultation, and with the stipulation that Maria undergo periodic drug testing, Rick agreed to participate. In a separate interview Maria also agreed and consented to drug testing, at least on a temporary basis.

This treatment plan was labor-intensive, requiring many hours of skilled therapeutic support. It was a much more expensive and demanding treatment plan than treating the child with medication and CBT for bipolar disorder. There were many challenges as the plan went forward. At the six-month mark, Dominic had resumed limited visitation with his mother and half-sister. Rick was better able to appreciate Dominic's feelings and needs in relation to Maria and Jenna, and Rick had established greater independence from his own mother. Dominic's eating had improved markedly. He slept through the night and his tantrums were better controlled and less frequent. There was no medication involved in the treatment, and Dominic's behavior was no longer suggestive of bipolar disorder. Indeed there was strong evidence that as the family conflicts were partly resolved and more consistency was brought to Dominic's attachment relationships, Dominic himself became better regulated and fundamentally more contented. The symptoms in this family system had largely shifted from Dominic to the ongoing difficulties between Rick and Maria in cooperating as parents, and it was in this dimension that ongoing therapeutic support was required.

Symptoms or Lived Experience

Previous authors have commented on the inadequacies of research in supporting the pediatric bipolar diagnosis, on the vagueness and imprecision of its criteria, on the absence of meaningful differential diagnostic considerations, on the economic forces advancing its adoption beyond the evidence of its science, and on its increasing application to children whose destabilization seems to relate primarily to the destabilization of their families and communities.[2]

Any number of factors can influence a child's behavior. These factors include the child's social history and the social history of the family; the child's cognitive and neurodevelopmental status, sense of secure attachment, self-value, and self-worth; the structure and organization of the child's immediate environment, sibling and peer relationships, and experiences at school; the quality of family connectedness and support; and the quality of the larger extended system of community in which the child develops.

One of the fundamental challenges to proper psychiatric diagnosis is the fact that it is often a time-consuming endeavor, requiring great skill and systematic attention to detail. Behavioral symptoms tend to overlap. Virtually identical behavioral symptoms can be caused by profoundly different factors. Gathering relevant and accurate historical information is difficult. There are, by and large, no definitive tests that can be administered in order to determine diagnosis, nor is direct examination of the child always definitive.

In the case of Dominic, the multiple causes of failed treatment are easy to see: excessively brief diagnostic procedures; the absence of differential considerations; the insistence on immediate, time-limited interventions and reductionist data as measures of response; and above all else, the failure to respond to attachment disruptions and social trauma as fundamental aspects of impaired development demanding insight, historical acknowledgment, and social repair.

These failings correspond precisely to critiques of the larger system of care. Perhaps one of the most interesting suggestions of this case study is that it is not so much the conscious decisions of expert providers that shape treatment, but rather the economic and administrative pressures of the system itself. In this sense our system of care is all too often unconsidered and unconscious.

Let's return to the question posed at the beginning of this paper: What was the fate of Dominic's experience in this system of care? Dominic's life was shaped by loss: the loss of his mother and of his sister. Attachment is fundamentally the most intense and demanding of memories. It is a conversation that begins before we can speak, and it retains its hold on us through moods and images, fluxes of thought and feeling that contain us as much as we contain them. Dominic's memory—his sense of himself in a continuing history—was no doubt disrupted not only by the sudden loss of his mother and sister, but also by the subsequent difficulties of his father in allowing Dominic's feelings of loss to persist and express themselves.

Lived experience is subtle because our histories extend from one generation to the next. Dominic's father had inherited and continued a familial discourse that bore the structure of "one good parent and one bad parent." Rick needed to enlist Dominic in his condemnation of Maria, and he needed Dominic to not long for her. That longing seemed to Rick a condemnation of his own parenting, threatening to reverse the binary logic by which, if he was not the good parent, he must be the bad parent. Dominic and Rick were engaged in a deeply unconscious struggle about the memory of

Maria and the possibility of her future return. Neither could win this struggle. And both suffered.

It took only a careful and skillful exploration of the family history to draw out these issues. Dominic's angry longing was just beneath the surface. It was a sign of strength, not weakness, and certainly not a sign of "bipolar disorder" that his memory and longing persisted.

From the beginning of this intervention, there was no attempt to make sense of Dominic's behavior. Instead, his unhappiness, tantrums, and refusals were attributed, without evidence, to neurobiological causes. He was encouraged to take a pill. The meaning of this act, perhaps lost to him at this age, will likely become apparent when he is older. In essence it says, "you have certain negative behaviors that make no sense and that signify an illness; we will cure them with medicine." That "illness" was nothing other than his persistent attachment to his mother.

Cognitive behavioral treatment played a similar role in this case. Dominic was instructed within a world view that insisted his genuine feelings were negative, unwanted, and in need of management. In effect, the attempt was made to enlist this child against his own mourning process and against his own cry for help. This fundamental turning of the child against himself became a demand of the treatment, and turned the meaning of treatment on its head. The child was placed under the requirement of exchanging his wounded subjectivity, his only true possession, for an objectification by social ideology and a conspiracy of forgetfulness. And when he failed to join with this debilitating attempt to manage himself, his diagnosis changed to a more severe category. The more this treatment approach failed, the more failure served as its justification.

This mode of treatment is a prescription for producing increasingly self-alienated children. As its objectifying habit of thought takes hold, we become impoverished. We lose the means of imagining ourselves, and most especially we lose the means of imagining our children, except in these impoverished terms.

8

An Invisible Plague: Pediatric Bipolar Disorder and the Chemical Colonization of Childhood

Daniel Burston

Buddha said: "Life is suffering." Although life is usually much more than suffering, no one disputes that it is integral to the human condition. Although painful and disconcerting, suffering is not always a *bad* thing, especially when viewed in retrospect. Suffering provides us with potent incentives and challenges to grow and develop, to mature, and to master fear and adversity. Yet nowadays much of children's suffering is hidden from public view and addressed indirectly—often by means of drug treatments that obscure the true source of their difficulties and rob them of important opportunities for growth and development.

THE NATURE OF HUMAN SUFFERING

To suffer is to endure bodily experiences and distressing states of mind that are impressed or imposed on us by circumstances that run contrary to our needs and desires, without our prior knowledge or consent. Suffering takes many forms, but most of them entail issues of *lack*, *loss*, or *conflict*.

Lack

Children may *lack* adequate nourishment, warmth, tactile stimulation, safety, security, or the kind of diligent parental involvement and oversight that shields them from noxious experiences of one sort or another. They may also lack an intact nervous system, immune system, and so on. These deficits may be brief and transient, deep and abiding, or unpredictable and episodic.

Loss

Loss is different from mere lack, because it entails the removal of a source of hope, comfort, or instruction that was formerly a palpable presence. Children can suffer the loss of a beloved parent, grandparent, friend, teacher, or cherished pet. They can also experience the loss of their physical or neurological integrity, popularity, self-esteem, trust in others, faith in the future, and so on. Whether these losses are irreversible or not depends in part on temperament, creativity, and the child's inner resolve. But above all, it depends on the presence of caring and insightful support from others, especially adults, to help a child rally, regroup, and move on.

Conflict

Children in distress often suffer from inner or interpersonal *conflicts* as well. Interpersonal conflicts pit them against significant others, transforming relationships that ought to be sources of psychic sustenance into dreary or frightening sources of tension, misunderstanding, and in worst-case scenarios, emotional or physical violence. Inner conflicts, which follow in the wake of interpersonal problems, are profoundly debilitating and potentially paralyzing because they provoke irreconcilable desires, attitudes, values, or beliefs, and the inability to choose definitively between them.

Three words—lack, loss, and conflict—cover the entire spectrum of human suffering. When a child suffers from severe or chronic deficits, profound loss, or painful inner or interpersonal conflicts, the distress and disorientation that he or she experiences as a result lead to thoughts, feelings, and behavior that make them candidates for a psychiatric diagnosis.

SUFFERING REINTERPRETED AS MENTAL ILLNESS

"Diagnosis" is a word many of us simply take for granted. It is something doctors perform as a prelude to recommending a course of treatment for a medical illness. Correct? Well, yes and no. The Greek word *gnosis* means knowledge, usually knowledge of an immediate and intuitive kind. The prefix *dia-*, which is also Greek, means "thorough, comprehensive, or encompassing." So by virtue of its etymological derivation, "diagnosis" *ought* to mean an encompassing knowledge or deep insight into the nature of a patient's malady. And if we are talking about children who are distressed or disturbed, the diagnosis would presumably also include an in-depth, empathic understanding of their developmental history and present familial and social circumstances, *in addition to* any medical problems they may be contending with. For Erik Erikson, author of *Childhood and Society*[1] and one of the most influential theorists in the field of child development, this is precisely what the term "diagnosis" meant. Erikson was a psychoanalyst steeped in history and the humanities. He thought deeply about the human life cycle, and was not wedded to the classifications of disorder used by conventional psychiatrists.[2]

DIAGNOSIS AND THE MEDICAL MODEL

Until recently, theorists such as Erikson helped shape how the average psychiatrist thought about children's emotional development.[3] This being so, the idea that a psychological crisis in childhood or adolescence might present a splendid opportunity to correct or deepen a child's development *without recourse to drugs* enjoyed considerable currency in the mental health professions. Indeed, when I began my clinical training, the vast majority of clinicians, when confronted by mental disorders of mild to moderate severity, seldom thought of medicating their patients. Medications were only used for cases of severe mental disorder. The question of whether or not to medicate arose only when psychosocial interventions, including psychotherapy, seemed out of the question or simply inadequate on their own. For most clinicians today, the question that immediately springs to mind is not whether or not to medicate, but which medication is the most appropriate. This question arises regardless of the age of the patient or severity of the disorder.

What social transformations occurred to make this dramatic change in outlook possible? One important factor is that since publication of the third edition of the American Psychiatric Association's *Diagnostic and Statistical Manual of Mental Disorders* (*DSM-III*) in 1980, psychiatry has divested itself of psychoanalytic habits of thought and practice, and as a result, the word "diagnosis" has come to mean a narrow and "objective" classification of illness, based on the clinician's ability to identify and enumerate the various signs and symptoms of a disease. The word "disease" is pivotal here because the underlying causes of a disorder are presumed to be traumas, deficits, or anomalies of a specifically *neurological* variety, even when interpersonal conflicts of one sort or another feature prominently in the patient's clinical profile and even though a clear-cut medical explanation for the alleged disorder has eluded researchers for more than a century (e.g., for diagnoses such as attention-deficit/hyperactivity disorder [ADHD] and depression). This one-sided emphasis on genetics and neurological causation renders the psychosocial dimensions of a child's disturbed and disturbing behavior all but irrelevant or inaccessible to the average clinician's gaze and seems to mandate chemical solutions, rendering psychosocial interventions—including therapy—secondary or superfluous.

PROLIFERATION OF DIAGNOSTIC CATEGORIES

Most psychiatrists feel that the profession's rejection of psychoanalysis and its return to the "medical model" represents a major advance in terms of objectivity. But there are dissenting voices as well. One cause for skepticism is the ceaseless proliferation of new categories of mental disorder.[4] In the U.S. Census of 1840, only one category of mental disorder was in use—namely, insanity. In 1880, however, census officials listed seven categories of mental disorder, in keeping with prevailing psychiatric opinion. The *International Classification of Diseases*, published by the World Health Organization (WHO) after World War II, listed ten categories of psychoses, nine psychoneuroses, and seven personality disorders, for a grand total of twenty-six categories.

Evidently, in the United States these criteria did not suffice; we do things on a grander scale. Accordingly, the first edition of the American Psychiatric Association's *Diagnostic and Statistical Manual of Mental Disorder* (DSM), published in 1952, contained 106 categories of mental disorder; the second edition, in 1968, listed 182. The third edition, in 1980, had 265; and the revised third edition, *DSM-III-R*, in 1987, had 292. The fourth edition, which appeared in 1993, includes almost 400, and many new categories are currently under consideration for *DSM-V*.[5]

In other words, within 150 years American psychiatry has either discovered—or in some sense, manufactured—almost 400 categories of mental disorder. And this total does not begin to reflect the potential number of variations of these diagnostic classifications wrought by the creation of the multiaxial diagnostic system for the *DSM-III-R*. If all of those specifications are taken into account, the diagnostic profiles available to clinicians number in the thousands. Sticking strictly to major categories, however, in the past century and a half, the average rate of increase is 25 new categories of mental disorder per decade, with "peak production" occurring between 1962 and 1993, when each successive edition of the DSM produced an average of 48 new categories, almost double the rate of the preceding century. Even Dr. Allen

Frances, who chaired the committee that produced the *DSM-IV*, expressed concern over "the wild growth and casual addition" of new mental disorders under the tenure of his predecessor, Dr. Robert Spitzer.[6]

Of course, not all psychiatrists feel that the *DSM* is horribly bloated, and when I have called attention to these trends in the past, psychiatrists frequently asked me why I object to the discovery and classification of new diseases—Isn't this what medical science is supposed to do? Doesn't this give psychiatry more leverage against unnecessary human suffering? The irony, of course, is that as things stand, there is no aspect of human experience brought on by lack, loss, or conflict (i.e., generic human suffering)—that cannot be interpreted (incorrectly) as the result of a specifically medical disorder. Moreover, when the real roots of suffering are ignored or addressed with inappropriate remedies, human suffering increases, rather than the reverse. Adding new categories indiscriminately simply widens the scope of the problem.

The unchecked proliferation of psychiatric categories is disturbing. An equally disturbing trend is the following: diagnostic categories that were formerly quite precise and circumscribed have been made more vague, inclusive, and all-encompassing, and categories that were formerly reserved for adolescents and adults are now being applied to children. Bipolar disorder (BD) is one such diagnosis.

PEDIATRIC BIPOLAR DISORDER

In contrast to many new diagnostic categories listed in the *DSM*, BD antedates the giddy and headlong inflation of the *DSM* by many decades. It was first described by German psychiatrist Emile Kraepelin in the 1890s. He characterized manic depression (as BD was then called) as long bouts of profoundly debilitating depression that are punctuated by bursts of frenzied activity accompanied by sleeplessness, grandiosity, recklessness, incoherence, and giddy euphoria, and that frequently escalate from odd or destructive behavior into frank psychosis. Depression punctuated by less florid symptoms of mania was termed "hypomania," and mania that was not followed by obvious depressive symptoms was simply called "mania."

Although the diagnostic criteria were revised several times, the epidemiological data on BD were remarkably consistent until ten years ago, and furnished one of the best reasons to give some credence to the medical model of mental disorder. The average age of onset for BD was between fifteen and forty-four years. It affected both sexes equally and afflicted between 0.5 and 1.5 percent of the general population across the globe. This dogged consistency across time and place strongly suggested that BD was strongly influenced by genetics.

This state of affairs started to change as the authors of the *DSM* expanded their classification to include four discrete versions of BD, each with its own unique profile. As a result, increasing numbers of people became candidates for a psychiatric diagnosis. Moreover, in the last few years, psychiatrists are claiming they can detect BD in *children as young as two or three years*, and they are medicating them accordingly.[7] In some instances, the child's symptoms conform more or less to the profile of "BD II." In others, it is claimed that the child's mood swings are so rapid and frequent that they defy classification according to any of the existing *DSM* criteria.[8]

Although epidemiological data for pediatric BD are still lacking, the Child and Adolescent Bipolar Foundation (CABF) nonetheless reports that the number of children diagnosed with BD is rising dramatically "as doctors begin to recognize the signs of the disorder in children." The CABF estimates conservatively that at "least three quarters of a million American children and teenagers—mostly undiagnosed—may currently suffer from bipolar disorder." In addition the CABF claims that

> it is suspected that a significant number of children diagnosed in the United States with attention-deficit disorder with hyperactivity (ADHD), have early-onset bipolar disorder instead of, or along with, ADHD. Depression in children and teens is usually chronic and relapsing. According to several studies, a significant proportion of the 3.4 million children and adolescents with depression in the United States may actually be experiencing the early onset of bipolar disorder, but have not yet experienced the manic phase of the illness.

Well, perhaps this is the case. But then again, the language on the CABF Web site describing the vast number of "as yet undiagnosed" bipolar children creates the confident expectation that this is not a rare childhood illness, paving the way for a self-fulfilling prophecy. Similarly, in their chapter for *Bipolar Disorders in Childhood*, researchers Lewinsohn, Seeley, and Klein state that "while there are no community data on the prevalence of what has been called prepubertal, juvenile, and pediatric bipolar disorder, it may be relatively common in clinically referred children."[9] And so once again, despite the manifest absence of compelling evidence, psychiatric authors create *an expectation* in the reader that BD is common in childhood.

Despite these uncertainties, pediatric BD is now an extremely popular diagnosis and is the subject of considerable media attention. Since the late 1990s, hundreds of research papers and several scholarly books have been published on the subject, whereas these were relatively uncommon only ten years ago. Meanwhile, cross-cultural comparisons reveal that prepubertal diagnoses of BD are rare in Germany and the Netherlands, but increasingly common in the United States, the only industrialized nation that fails to provide universal health care and maternity leave, and which has in general the weakest policies in support of children's welfare and environmental protection. Can this be coincidence? Moreover, research indicates that the antidepressants and stimulants that are prescribed with such frequency in the United States actually *exacerbate* the many behavioral disturbances labeled "early-onset bipolar disorder."

For many mental health professionals, the proliferation of diagnoses of pediatric BD is cause for concern. As a result, some modest steps have been taken to stem the tide. Guidelines recently issued jointly by the CABF and the American Academy of Child and Adolescent Psychiatry (AACAP) stipulate that children under the age of six should *not* be given this diagnosis under any circumstances.[10] In an editorial in the *Journal of the American Academy of Child and Adolescent Psychiatry*, where these guidelines were unveiled, Dr. John McLennan wrote: "Labeling severe tantrums in toddlers as major mental illness lacks face validity and undermines the credibility of our profession."[11]

These guidelines are a beginning, but they do not eliminate all cause for concern because they are not mandatory or binding in any way; they are merely recommendations. They stress the importance of clarifying the frequency, intensity, number, and duration of symptoms, but they remind clinicians, for example, that "hot, hungry, stressed and/or tired children without psychopathology may become irritable." Likewise, clinicians are admonished that grandiose statements—such as "I am Superman!"—are not necessarily indicative of mental disorder, depending on the child's age.[12]

One problem with these guidelines is that they hinge entirely on the description and enumeration of symptoms. Although clinicians are not actually forbidden from considering the possibility that symptoms may often have a hidden meaning (or that the children who behave in these ways are trying to *communicate* something in some desperate, disjointed fashion), these theoretical or interpretive options are not even mentioned in passing. The overarching presumption is that children's symptoms are rooted in neurological losses or deficits, which are the true source of all their inner and interpersonal (i.e., "behavioral") issues. Once such an assumption is made, careful consideration of the developmental, social, and cultural contexts of children's lives are no longer integral or even much relevant to the diagnosis, as though profound psychic disturbance is merely a disease like the flu or the measles. It is also disturbing that McLellan and Kowatch are clearly concerned that many child psychiatrists have forgotten what it is like to be a hot or hungry child or to feel that one is invincible (e.g., Superman).

The most troubling aspect of these guidelines is that they promote the practice of using multiple prescriptions—*polypharmacy*—to treat children and adolescents whose behavior is disturbing to adults. They recommend that if the first drug the psychiatrist prescribes does not work, then after a certain interval of time, another drug should be tried, and then another, and another, and so on, until the child is "stable." The guidelines never even hint at the possibility that the initial course of drug treatment might be ineffective because *the original diagnosis was actually incorrect, and should be revised or discarded.* Rather, the clinician is charged with finding the right medication or combination of medications. Furthermore, these recommendations fail to acknowledge, much less account for, the fact that no research evidence to date proves that polypharmacy is any more effective than *monotherapy*—the use of a single pharmacological agent.[13]

In a recent article titled "How I Learned to Stop Worrying and Love the *DSM*," psychiatrist Philip M. Sinaikin recounts his clinical work with a seventeen-year-old female whom we shall call Kate: she was hospitalized for depression, self-destructive behaviors, and vague suicidal thoughts, and received a diagnosis of BD and prescriptions for *three medications*—a mood stabilizer, an antidepressant, and an antipsychotic.[14] Because of Kate's fragile emotional condition, it was decided that she should not return to school, despite the fact that she had earned a 3.5 GPA and had a combined SAT score of 1590—a remarkable achievement that prompted many colleges and universities to solicit applications from her *before* she graduated from high school.

Careful questioning did not disclose any prior history of bipolar or even hypomanic behavior, and when asked why she was given this diagnosis, the patient replied that it was probably because she acknowledged having "mood swings" on a symptom checklist. When asked what was troubling her, Kate complained that she could not handle the stress of her senior project in high school and was distressed at the prospect of going away to college the following year. Further inquiry disclosed that she had no social life to speak of and had never been on a date.

Rather than accept Kate's diagnosis at face value, Dr. Sinaikin wisely revised the "story line" underlying her "case" in order to render Kate's distress intelligible to herself and to others by instilling a sense of agency and opportunity, rather than victimization, in his patient. Instead of narrating her difficulties in terms of a lifelong medical disability, he construed it developmentally as being the result of a temporary lack of social skills, and socioculturally as a lack of being valued for her academic achievements. In terms of our initial reflections, he interpreted Kate's suffering as the result of two types of lack, without attributing her problems to an underlying disease. He took her off the mood stabilizer and the antipsychotic medications and urged her to return to high school and apply for college. She promptly won a four-year scholarship and embarked on her undergraduate degree. Summing up this case, Dr. Sinaikin concluded:

> I am not arguing that psychiatric illness does not exist, nor am I opposed to the use of psychotropic medication, but I do believe that diagnostic labels and medications should be used judiciously and within the context of an appropriate narrative. Renarrativizing *DSM* story lines can be exhausting work and sometimes meets with significant resistance, but overall, I believe it can be a successful and rewarding approach for the many clinicians who struggle with the reductionistic and impersonal *DSM* medical model that we are faced with today.

It is instructive to note that Dr. Sinaikin's approach to treatment—"narrative therapy theory"—does not privilege or dismiss the medical model, but treats it simply as *one interpretive option among others*, including the existential, developmental, sociocultural, psychoanalytic, spiritual, and interpersonal perspectives, all of which have merit in his eyes.

Dr. Sinaikin also notes that narrative therapy theory is closely allied to and inspired by social constructivism, a philosophical movement that is predicated on the ideas that

- Realities are constructed and constituted through language.
- Realities are maintained and organized through language.
- There are no essential truths.

According to social constructivism, psychiatric labels are not neutral scientific terms that accurately describe an objectively existing disturbance. On the contrary, the disturbance itself is a social construction. By this account, diagnoses often become self-fulfilling prophesies, actively shaping in adverse ways the life and destiny of those so labeled. When deployed in this fashion, the *DSM* generates new narrative identities, or perhaps *pseudo-identities*, that patients then live out as existential truths. This is not the result of disinterested scientific research, says Sinaikin, but of an unconscious process of reification in which concepts, ideas and abstractions . . . are literally transformed into what appear to be objectively valid realities grounded in the immutable laws of nature. Thus, "rapid-cycling bipolar disorder" moves from the realm of the concept to concrete reality by the processes of reification, supported by the established institution of psychiatry and legitimized by what is presented as scientific research. From a social constructivist perspective, psychiatrists do not need to prove whether bipolar disorder is a brain disease or whether someone has the disease, because those who are labeled and treated as bipolar will, for all intents and purposes, be bipolar.

Dr. Sinaikin's constructivist philosophy is not merely a critical tool, however. It is rooted in a strong sense of the clinician's obligation to provide patients with narratives that increase their sense of agency and self-authorship (nowadays termed "empowerment") and diminish their actual or potential experience of vulnerability and victimization at the hands of others. With these thoughts in mind, Sinaikin invites us to imagine

a 4-year-old rambunctious child presenting to the authority of the psychiatrist and emerging with the label of BD (bipolar disorder). Not only would the child's sense of self form around that label, [but] the surrounding reality will support and confirm it. Teachers, parents, school counselors, police officers will now respond to this child based on their understanding of how a person with BD acts and should be handled.

Dr. Sinaikin's troubling scenario provokes reflection on the ill effects of a thoughtless diagnosis for a child who is stressed or poorly socialized, but still neurologically intact. Given the child's youth and plasticity, whatever he or she currently lacks in terms of appropriate attachment and parental care, clear rules, and boundaries and so on, can presumably be remedied in time to avert any permanent ill effects—in principle, anyway. But without quite saying so, Sinaikin implies that a misdiagnosis of BD forecloses on this possibility, robbing children of their future. Why? Because children who believe that they suffer from a lifelong disability act accordingly, and grow up with brains that are burdened by toxic drugs.

Dr. Sinaikin's caution against an excessive or ideological reliance on the medical model is welcome, but hardly new. Ever since the late 1950s, sociologists such as Erving Goffman and Thomas Scheff have shown that the diagnosis of a severe mental disorder often constitutes an induction ceremony, whereby a child or adolescent is launched on a career as a lifelong mental patient.[15] Very often, the real or alleged disorder becomes the core, or the pivot, of their identity, and the perfect excuse for ducking the challenges and responsibilities of a more mature existence.[16] In short, the label is socially and psychologically disfiguring, a license for immaturity, as well as a potential hazard to the growing child's brain.

The question becomes the following: How prevalent or widespread are these instances of misdiagnosis? They are very common, by some accounts. Psychiatrist Joseph Goldberg, of the Zucker Hillside Hospital in Glen Oaks, New York, states that nearly half of patients suffering from manic depression, or BD, may have been abused as children. In a recent issue of the *British Journal of Psychiatry*, Goldberg said that emotional, physical, and sexual abuse are all linked with dramatic mood swings and changes in behavior. In his own words: "Our results suggest that a history of severe childhood abuse is to be found in approximately half of adults with bipolar disorder." Indeed, a third of the patients in Goldberg's study suffered from *multiple* forms of abuse. But in the kinds of cursory evaluations that most such cases receive, these facts are suppressed, and if uncovered, they are either denied or minimized in the interests of "normalizing" the appearance of the family because of the embarrassment, stigma, and potential legal entanglements and sanctions that might ensue if these matters were not swept under the rug.

Child psychiatrist Mary Burke offers a somewhat different explanation for the dramatic increase of bipolar diagnoses among children. In her judgment, severely depressed mothers are emotionally and sometimes physically unavailable to their infants, which in turn can lead to "insecure attachment" and chronic anxiety. If these fretful, insecurely attached infants also have naturally sensitive temperaments and are therefore more difficult to soothe than the average baby, their depressed mothers are more likely to perceive these traits as evidence of disturbance, leading them to retreat even further from their infants and causing even more rupture in the mother–infant attachment that is so critical for their infants' mental health. As their children's signals of distress mount—marked by tantrums, incessant crying, and irritability—the mothers, who are themselves overwhelmed by their own unmet emotional needs, may seek consultation with a psychiatrist who validates their concerns that their children have a psychiatric illness. Burke also hypothesizes that in general, children have difficulty regulating their moods in the face of chronic parental stress or ineptitude. If children's emotional lives become overwhelming and unmanageable to their parents, they are at much higher risk of being labeled bipolar.

Burke's remarks about the social and interpersonal roots of severe mood dysregulation in infancy and childhood are consistent with a robust and rapidly growing research literature that stresses the importance of early attachment and attunement of parent to child as guarantor of mood stability.[17] Significantly, references to this impressive body of work are conspicuously absent in the growing literature on pediatric BD. This being so, it is important to emphasize that early losses, deficits and conflicts between young children and their parents can render the children emotionally overwhelmed, immature, and less able to regulate, express, or contain their feelings, which then erupt in ways that resemble BD.

STEMMING THE TIDE OF MISDIAGNOSES

Ever since Kraepelin's work in the 1890s, BD has been widely understood to be a genetically linked neurological illness. Very few of those who suffer from it, or those close to them, doubt its potentially devastating effects. Given that this is so, it is alarming that so many children are being labeled as bipolar when their symptoms (1) usually do not fit the typical clinical profiles for this disorder; and (2) can often be understood more parsimoniously as the result of neglect or abuse. Why is this happening? Dr. Sinaikin suggests that many psychiatrists are so strongly committed to the medical model that they simply will not entertain alternative interpretations, or "narratives." Although the pervasive reluctance to reckon with other possibilities is usually justified on scientific (or *pseudoscientific*) grounds, there are also many *nonscientific* reasons why practitioners adhere to the medical model. Given the prevailing regime of managed care and the powerful influence of the pharmaceutical industry, many psychiatrists simply lack the time, training, or practical incentives to complete a thorough psychosocial evaluation of each child and family or to provide psychotherapy or family therapy, if these are called for. If psychiatrists are courageous and conscientious enough to go this route, they may court the disapproval and ostracism of their colleagues, and forfeit the substantial financial perks that come with prescribing drugs in a routine and injudicious manner.

Another nonscientific factor that influences the judgment of psychiatrists is parental or familial pressure. Many families are experiencing a great deal of stress because funding for programs that support parents and communities has been slashed in recent years.[18] In addition, the number and quantity of pollutants being released into the environment that demonstrably undermine brain development has increased dramatically.[19] Moreover, efforts to reform the public school system through "No Child Left Behind" often ignore children's developmental needs,[20] whereas media presentations, which exert a powerful impact on children's minds, grow more violent and toxic by the day.[21] In the present cultural climate, it is intrinsically difficult to raise children to wholesome maturity, and many stressed, beleaguered parents whose faltering efforts do not succeed may *prefer* to imagine that their children suffer from a neurological disorder rather than ponder the Herculean task of reforming a system that has failed them, or admit to any personal failure to properly nourish, protect, or guide their offspring. Moreover, many parents are encouraged in this direction by mental health professionals, and they are often misinformed about the potential side effects of the medications prescribed to their children.[22]

On reflection, it is sometimes the case that in delivering a diagnosis of pediatric BD, a child psychiatrist is merely colluding with parents in their effort to avert their attention from these deeply disconcerting scenarios. Although it may afford some short-term relief, this avoidance strategy then becomes part of the problem. Americans are experiencing a series of concurrent and overlapping crises with respect to parenting, education, and environmental sustainability—crises that are expressed in increasing numbers of distressed and disruptive youngsters whose behavior disappoints and antagonizes adult caretakers, both inside and outside of the home. Rather than tackling these systemic issues by drafting and supporting new laws and policies that protect children and support parents, we "treat" children on a case-by-case basis under the auspices of the medical model. In other words, we search for individually calibrated chemical solutions to what are predominantly *social* problems. This expedient appeals to the individualistic American mind-set and its longstanding cultural romance with the quick chemical "fix" for problems. But on deeper reflection, this approach is deeply irrational, with the potential to backfire dangerously if we don't wake up to such folly.

Moreover, those who are versed in the history of psychiatry have an eerie sense of *déjà vu* about these developments. For example, U.S. psychiatrists in the 1950s started to use the "schizophrenia" diagnosis in a reckless and cavalier fashion. In fact, they were three to four times more likely to label someone schizophrenic than their British counterparts, which caused no end of transatlantic controversy, as careful British psychiatrists scolded their profligate American cousins.[23]

These facts are well known. What is less well known is that the alleged "epidemic" of schizophrenia in the United States furnished the pretext necessary for psychiatrists to try out a new class of drugs, called *phenothiazines*, on this bumper crop of newly diagnosed patients.[24] Robert Whitaker, author of *Mad in America*, points out that in the late nineteenth century, when the drugs were first invented, phenothiazines were used chiefly as industrial dyes and later, in the

1930s, as insecticides or agents to kill parasites in swine. At that time, no one imagined that these drugs had medicinal value. When the market for them vanished new applications were sought, and the discovery that phenothiazines could function as "chemical straightjackets" created a bonanza for drug companies.[25]

Who else benefited from this dramatic market expansion? Certainly not patients! A recent WHO study indicates that the average person's chances of complete recovery from schizophrenia is actually much higher in countries that are too poor to provide their populations with these medications. By contrast, someone who starts on phenothiazines—or on other "atypical antipsychotics"—stands an 80 percent chance of undergoing repeated breakdowns and hospitalizations (the infamous "revolving door syndrome"). These data—whose integrity has stood up to repeated criticism and scrutiny from the mental health professions—would prompt any rational person to conclude that in the average case, taking phenothiazines is more likely to hinder than to help a psychotic person recover, at least in the long run.[26]

While the introduction of phenothiazines in the 1950s furnishes an ominous parallel to our present predicament, notable differences between the 1950s and today's difficult situation render the plight of children even more worrisome. When U.S. psychiatry diagnosed schizophrenics by the bushel in the 1950s, *pharmacological remedies were still considered the treatment of last resort*. If all else failed, medications were tried. Nowadays, however, pharmacological remedies are widely considered to be the first and best treatment option, a fact that is reflected in policy statements of the Bush Administration, as well as the psychiatric and drug lobbies.[27] Indeed, if the FDA's behavior is any indication, the prevailing attitude in the mental health industry and in society at large is that a new pharmacological agent is presumed "innocent" (harmless) until proven otherwise. This being so, it is instructive to note that the Greek word *pharmakos* means "poison" as well as "medicine," and the presumption that a newly synthesized compound is "innocent" or harmless is a gross injustice to consumers, especially when the consumers are children, who unlike their adult counterparts, never seek these treatments voluntarily and lack both the skills to evaluate and the power to refuse such harmful medications. And in the process, we are *normalizing* the use of powerful psychotropic agents in children, whose brains are still fragile and unformed.

On a societal level, we might compare the increasingly routine drugging of children with the normalization of doping in professional sport. In both instances, drugging is used to increase performance or to compensate for perceived weaknesses, and it is becoming standard practice. The difference, of course, is that athletes are usually adults who give their more or less informed consent when they are drugged.

It is a Faustian bargain because, in the long run, they harm themselves by doping. But in the short run, they derive considerable social and financial rewards in exchange for playing along. Finally, what they do is illegal, and although extremely prevalent in sporting circles, doping is still opposed by large sections of the sports community, who are calling for more screening and tougher sanctions, and rightly so.

Unlike athletes, young children cannot weigh the risks and benefits of taking drugs, and they are powerless to refuse them. Moreover, although the reckless use of polypharmacy is like an invisible plague that claims increasing numbers of children every year, very few people are actively opposed to the present state of affairs, and the use of excessive and inappropriate medication is perfectly legal. In instances such as these, the child gains nothing. Only *others* profit. The child who is wrongly medicated is a hapless victim in an elaborate charade of abuse, neglect, and quasi-scientific labeling on the part of family, teachers, and mental health professionals.

In cases of real or alleged pediatric BD, the treatment of choice more often than not is the newer atypical antipsychotics in conjunction with mood stabilizers. The toxic side effects of these drugs were hidden behind a dense fog of industry hype until relatively recently.[28] The only certain benefits that accrue from their routine usage go to the drug companies that manufacture and sell them at an obscene profit, with the support of state and federal governments. Although the rhetoric of psychiatry emphasizes the subtlety and complexity of clinical judgment and the need to tailor the treatment to the needs of the individual patient, the fact remains that the federal government has encouraged Texas, Pennsylvania, Ohio, and other states to legislate specific treatment protocols for specific diagnoses: protocols that stipulate precisely which drugs are to be used and in what circumstances. Although these protocols, called "medical algorithms," purport to be "evidence-based" or supported by "expert consensus," the so-called experts who compose such panels are invariably industry insiders paid handsome sums for spinning the evidence favorably for "Big Pharma" and for ignoring the abundant evidence of the potential of these same drugs to do harm.[29]

We therefore face the inevitable question: Are the "early detection techniques"—promulgated by the CABF, AACAP, and the many clinicians who diagnose and treat even earlier and more aggressively than their guidelines mandate—based on sound scientific research? Or are they a subtle and ingenious strategy to open up new markets for drug companies? When all of the evidence is weighed carefully, it points strongly to the latter conclusion. Indeed, future generations may look back on the early twenty-first century as an era when the chemical colonization of childhood really began in earnest, although whether they would view these developments positively or negatively remains to be seen and may depend on whether we act now. The questions become the following: Will we act in time? Will we have sufficient impact to stem the tide of misdiagnoses? Such questions are difficult to answer. The situation has reached such a pitch that many psychiatrists who are wary or opposed to these trends are quite afraid to speak out, fearing reprisals of one sort or another. They have reason to be fearful. Careers have been ruined or lost for this kind of candor. David Healy's firing and abrupt divestiture from the University of Toronto's Department of Psychiatry is a disturbing case in point (although Healy was fired because he spoke out against indiscriminate use of SSRIs, especially for teens, rather than against the drugs that are prescribed for pediatric BD).[30] Closer to home, Dr. Stephan Kruszewski, a Harvard-trained psychiatrist in Harrisburg, Pennsylvania, was fired from Pennsylvania's Department of Public Welfare for speaking out against state-sanctioned polypharmacy and the deepening collusion among government, psychiatry, and Big Pharma, which is mandated by the Pennsylvania Medical Algorithm Project.[31]

THE POLITICS OF DIAGNOSIS

In many instances, unfortunately, a psychiatric diagnosis masks rather than reveals the real roots of children's suffering. So what do we do? Dispense with diagnosis altogether? Continue with business as usual? Reintroduce the psychoanalytic ideas and practices that psychiatry abandoned in the diagnostic arena? Let us address these proposals one at a time.

When considering children who have symptoms that resemble BD in adults, we have much to learn from pediatrician Mel Levine's approach to treating learning disabilities. Dr. Levine has demonstrated that learning disabilities, which allegedly result from underlying neurological abnormalities, are remedied more effectively when they are framed as *different styles of learning* (each with its own specific strengths and weaknesses), rather than being framed as *medical diseases*. After all, the medical approach to mental illness presupposes a model of a "normal" brain that, from an empirical standpoint, is no more than a heuristic fiction. And even if there are neurological components or underpinnings to a specific learning problem, as Dr. Levine says, an inordinate emphasis on them makes those so labeled feel that they are not up to doing as well as others or as well and they could and should do. In short, emphasis on the neurological components becomes a self-attribution that becomes a self-fulfilling prophecy.[34]

Dr. Levine describes himself as an existentialist rather than a constructivist, but if we disregard the philosophical nuances and focus on commonalities, he obviously shares Dr. Sinaikin's ethical concern for providing patients with an overall assessment of their own skills and situation that stimulates their optimism and sense of personal agency, rather than a global sense of inadequacy that promotes passivity and lowered self-esteem. Unfortunately, however, when it comes to more severe behavioral problems, the call to abolish diagnosis altogether is impractical. Whether or not pediatric BD per se actually exists, many children suffer from brain disorders that stem from profound emotional deprivation in infancy, or from exposure to toxic pollutants such as lead and mercury that are known to compromise brain development.[35] When this is the case, simply developing new story lines to help children organize their identities and build self-esteem (à la Sinaikin or Levine) is not an adequate response.

Perhaps we should stick to "business as usual" and continue to revise, refine, and expand the *DSM*. But this won't work. As pointed out earlier, the *DSM* is already intolerably bloated. We need to think about how to shrink the *DSM* without losing the proverbial baby with the bath water. To do this effectively, we must be able to discriminate between what is "baby" and what is "bathwater." To this end, we should declare an immediate and binding moratorium on the adoption of new categories, including pediatric BD, and reflect at length about the contexts in which different diagnostic categories emerged historically. Furthermore, clinicians who have benefited financially from a long professional association with large pharmaceutical companies should be excluded from the committees that review and revise existing criteria. Otherwise, we'll just repeat and intensify the errors of the past.

Should we go back to the days when psychoanalysis dominated psychiatric thinking? In some ways, this proposal is quite appealing. For one thing, analytically oriented clinicians are instructed early in their training that as treatment proceeds and the patient improves, it is prudent to revisit, revise, or completely discard their original diagnosis. Indeed, training analysts generally insist that a full and accurate diagnosis—that is, a deep and encompassing knowledge of the patient's inner and interpersonal worlds—is generally somewhat elusive until the final phase of treatment, when the roots of the patient's deepest and earliest developmental disturbances finally surface for interpretation and reflection. Consequently, the idea of changing a patient's diagnosis two or three times in the course of treatment is not novel or aversive to the seasoned analyst.

By contrast, when treating a patient within the medical model, the psychiatrist generally arrives at a "correct" diagnosis *before* treatment begins and then tends to "lock in" to that diagnosis. Furthermore, under managed care, psychiatrists are often under enormous institutional and financial pressure to render a diagnosis swiftly; they often do so in a matter of minutes. However, once one has surveyed the world of mental disorder through psychoanalytic lenses, the idea that a thorough and accurate diagnostic appraisal can be based on checklists or on the mechanical enumeration of clinical symptoms and signs in the interval of less than an hour, seems superficial at best.

Yet despite the benefits of an approach to assessment that does not focus exclusively on symptoms or valorize drug treatment alone, problems remain because there exists not one but dozens of schools of psychoanalysis, each of which favors different developmental theories and diagnostic criteria. Theoretical differences between the various schools are notoriously impervious to arguments based on empirical research, prompting critics to liken psychoanalysis to a kind of secular religion, complete with dogma, schisms, and so on.[36] Although we cannot embrace psychoanalysis wholeheartedly, we cannot reject it completely either. It reminds us that (1) symptoms may have unconscious or inarticulate meanings in addition to neurobiological causes; and (2) if clinicians' efforts to be objective are not balanced by strong attunement to their own needs and feelings and to those of their patients, they will fail them in some crucial respects. Ideally, we would distill what is best in psychoanalytic practice and reconfigure the economic and institutional arrangements that shape and constrain the delivery of mental health services so that diagnosis can be practiced in a thorough and humane way.

CONCLUSION

When the suffering of young patients results chiefly from interpersonal or cultural deficits, losses, or traumas, the summary invocation of the medical model to sanction reckless pharmacological interventions is not merely one way of understanding or addressing the patient, as Dr. Sinaikin suggests. In a real and disturbing sense, it is a way of *not* understanding patients; a way of averting attention from the social, interpersonal, and environmental dimensions of their suffering. Such an approach to diagnosis sanctions a callous indifference to the circumstances that provoke and sustain the problematic behavior of the patients, and is therefore more likely to hinder than to assist them in converting their experience into an opportunity for reevaluating and redefining themselves and furthering their personal development.

The solution to the current crisis in child psychiatry is not to jettison completely the disease model of mental disorder. There are instances in

in the number of children with neuropsychological disturbances, which are now estimated to be as high as one in six.[1] An expert committee from the U.S. National Research Council concluded that 3 percent of neurodevelopmental disabilities are the direct result of environmental exposure to such poisons and that another 25 percent arise through interactions between environmental exposures and genetic susceptibility.[2] But these statistics were based on the impact of the very small number of environmental poisons that have already been tested, and the numbers could rise sharply if research were extended to all of the chemical exposures of the developing human brain. It is striking that the mental health community has virtually ignored the health risks to children growing up in a world that is awash with thousands of synthetic chemicals, hundreds of which are already known to be poisonous to the brain.

This chapter is a "call to research" the role that prenatal and early childhood exposure to neurotoxic industrial chemicals might be playing in the American pediatric mental health crisis in general and in the childhood bipolar epidemic specifically. The recently launched *National Children's Study* (available at www.nationalchildrensstudy.gov)—funded by the U.S. Department of Health and Human Services through the National Institutes of Health and the Centers for Disease Control and Prevention and by the U.S. Environmental Protection Agency—will examine the effects of a wide range of environmental influences on the health and development of more than 100,000 children across the United States, following them from before birth until the age of twenty-one. This unprecedented study, which is already slated to track cognitive and neurobehavioral skills as well as neurodevelopmental disabilities, offers an ideal opportunity for a long overdue partnership between the mental health and environmental health research communities.

The sections that follow elucidate why the developing brain is uniquely vulnerable to toxic assault, summarize what is currently known about the effects of exposure to neurotoxic industrial chemicals, and consider how these chemicals may be important contributors to the recent surge in children's psychological disturbances.

VULNERABILITY OF THE DEVELOPING BRAIN

The developing human brain is inherently much more susceptible to injury than the adult brain.[3] The brain begins as a small strip of cells along the back of the embryo that develops, over the next nine months, into a complex organ of billions of precisely located, highly interconnected, specialized cells. Optimal brain development requires that neurons move along precise pathways from their points of origin to their assigned locations, establish connections with other cells both nearby and distant, and learn to communicate with other cells via such connections. All of these processes must take place within a tightly controlled time frame in which each developmental stage must be reached on schedule and in the correct sequence.[4]

Because of the extraordinary complexity of human brain development, windows of unique susceptibility to toxic interference arise that have no counterpart in the mature brain or in any other organ. If a developmental process in the brain is halted or inhibited, there is little potential for later repair and the consequences can therefore be permanent.[5] During fetal development, the placenta offers some protection against unwanted chemical exposures, but it is not an effective barrier against many environmental pollutants.[6] For example, many metals easily cross the placenta, and the concentration of mercury in umbilical cord blood is often substantially higher than in maternal blood.[7] The blood-brain barrier, which protects the adult brain from many toxic chemicals, is not completely formed until about six months after birth.[8]

The human brain continues to develop after birth, and the period of heightened vulnerability therefore extends over many months, through infancy and into early childhood. Although most brain cells have been formed by the time of birth, growth of glial cells and myelinization of axons continues for several years.[9]

The susceptibility of infants and children—relative to that of adults—to industrial chemicals is further enhanced by their increased exposures, augmented absorption rates, and diminished ability to detoxify their bodies.[10] Persistent organic pollutants, including many pesticides and PCBs, accumulate in breast tissue and are passed on to the infant via breast milk, resulting in infant exposure that exceeds the mother's own exposure by a hundredfold.[11]

Although severe neurological damage as a result of a high-dose exposure to a chemical poison is most likely to be detected and documented, careful follow-up research typically uncovers a dose-dependent range of toxic effects, including subclinical effects at low doses.[12] The classic example is the subclinical effect of lead exposure, as demonstrated by the research I conducted with Herbert Needleman. We showed that although exposure to low doses of lead may not cause acute toxicity, it nonetheless may reduce intelligence and lead to subtle changes in behavior, with profound consequences for individual children and for society at large. Our work has been confirmed by large-scale epidemiological studies.[13] Animal studies support the notion that a wide range of industrial chemicals can cause developmental neurotoxicity at low doses that are not harmful to mature animals.[14] Such injury seems to result in permanent changes in brain function that might become detectable only when the animal reaches maturity. Because developmental neurotoxicity might not be apparent from routine toxicology tests,[15] identification of neurotoxic chemicals often rests on clinical and epidemiological data.

AN OVERVIEW OF NEUROTOXIC INDUSTRIAL CHEMICALS

This section lists and describes all of the environmental chemicals that have been shown through research to be toxic to the human brain (excluding drugs, food additives, microbial toxins, snake venoms, and similar biogenic substances or substances that have been shown only in laboratory animals to b neurotoxic). This list is without question an underrepresentation of the actual number of chemicals that can damage the brain; the vast majority have not been tested, particularly with regard to their effects on the developing brain. Most of the substances that have been tested are metals, solvents, and pesticides.

Lead

The neurotoxic effects of lead in adults were known in ancient Rome but a report from Australia one hundred years ago was the first description of epidemic lead poisoning in young children; the source of the outbreak was traced to lead-based paint ingested by children playing on verandas with peeling paint.[16] Further reports of childhood lead poisoning from the United States and Europe followed. Lead poisoning was thought at that time to be an acute illness, from which a child either recovered or died. Long-term effects were first documented in the 1940s, when nineteen of twenty survivors of acute poisoning were noted to have severe learning and behavioral problems.[17]

Despite those early pediatric warnings, the largely unchecked use of lead in gasoline, paints, ceramic glazes, and many other products through much of the twentieth century caused continued risk of lead poisoning. During the 1970s widespread subclinical neurobehavioral deficits—including problems with concentration, memory, cognition, and behavior—were documented in asymptomatic children with raised blood-lead concentrations.[18] Spurred by recommendations issued by the European Regional Office of the World Health Organization, studies were initiated in many countries. The results corroborated the previous conclusions.[19]

As a result of accumulating evidence, many sources of lead exposure became controlled, although not all sources and not in all countries. A 90-percent reduction in childhood blood–lead concentrations followed the termination of lead additives in gasoline.[20] Newer research into lead neurotoxicity has focused on the shape of the dose-response curve at very low exposures that seem to cause surprisingly large functional decrements.[21] As compelling evidence came pouring in, health agencies worldwide reduced the permissible concentration of lead in children's blood. However, current research[22] suggests that these guidelines need to be even more stringent.

Methylmercury

Developmental toxicity of methylmercury became evident in the 1960s in Minamata, Japan, where an epidemic of spasticity, blindness, and profound mental retardation was seen in infants born to mothers who consumed fish from contaminated waters. After many years of clinical and experimental studies, the source proved to be mercury compounds released into Minamata Bay by a plastics plant.[23] Similar outbreaks of profound neurodevelopmental disorders in the infants of seemingly unaffected mothers have arisen after maternal consumption during pregnancy of seed grain that had been treated with methylmercury fungicides.[24] Studies of a serious poisoning incident in Iraq established a crude dose–response association between mercury concentration in maternal hair and risk of neurological abnormalities in the women's children.[25]

Recent studies have focused on prenatal exposures to moderate concentrations of methylmercury, typical of populations who have diets that include a high intake of seafood and freshwater fish contaminated with methylmercury. A prospective study of a community in New Zealand that met this criteria exhibited a three-point decrement in IQ and emotional changes in children born to women with mercury concentration in their hair of greater than 6 mg/g.[26] Another prospective study in the Faroe Islands noted evidence of dose-related impairments in memory, attention, language, and visuospatial perception in exposed children.[27] And a third prospective study in the Seychelles indicated that prenatal exposure to methylmercury caused by the mothers' heavy consumption of ocean fish damaged the developing brain.[28] A number of cross-sectional studies recorded significant associations between methylmercury exposure and neurobehavioral impairment in young children.[29]

The U.S. National Academy of Sciences reviewed the previously cited research and concluded that strong evidence exists for fetal neurotoxicity of methylmercury, even at low exposures.[30] These findings have led food safety authorities to issue dietary advisories; national and international agencies (coordinated by the U.N. Environment Programme) now seek to control and restrict the release of mercury to the environment. Substantial reductions have already been achieved in mercury use and release from hospitals and incinerators.[31] A related substance, ethylmercury, has been widely used as a preservative in vaccines, but neurotoxic risk has not been documented.[32]

Arsenic

The first report that arsenic causes damage to children's developing brains was published in Japan in 1955, after powdered milk contaminated with arsenic led to more than 12,000 cases of poisoning and 131 deaths.[33] A follow-up study of three groups of adolescents born during this period included one group that was fully breast-fed, one that was exposed to the tainted milk product, and one that received other supplements but no tainted formula.[34] Compared with national rates, a tenfold increase in mentally retarded individuals was seen in the tainted milk group.[35] Poor school records, emotional disturbances, or borderline electroencephalogram findings were also more common in the exposed group. Several cross-sectional studies of school-age children report similar findings.[36] And yet, despite the fact that research has established its toxicity to the developing brain, arsenic is not well regulated and is present in groundwater worldwide.

Polychlorinated Biphenyls

Polychlorinated biphenyls (PCBs) were widely used as insulators in electrical equipment until the 1970s, when they were found to be toxic to humans.[37] However, they were not known to cause brain damage until children in Taiwan were exposed prenatally, when cooking oil was accidentally contaminated by PCBs during manufacturing. The exposed children were subsequently found to have low birth weight, delayed developmental milestones, and lower IQ in comparison with unexposed siblings.[38] A follow-up study showed growth impairment, slow development, lack of endurance, clumsy movement, and very low IQs.[39]

According to epidemiological studies in the United States, populations who were exposed prenatally to PCBs through maternal diet exhibited an average IQ score that was 6.2 points below the IQ of children with lower exposures at age eleven.[40] Research in Holland and Germany also found intellectual deficits in children after PCB exposures.[41] Although PCB manufacture has been banned in most nations and exposures are decreasing, PCBs remain in the environment at concentrations sufficiently high to damage developing brains.[42]

Solvents

It is a well-established fact that heavy, long-term consumption of ethanol (the active ingredient in alcoholic drinks) can lead to serious and permanent brain damage, including Wernicke's syndrome. Fetal alcohol syndrome includes intellectual and behavioral deficits and changes in facial features. Even when a pregnant woman has consumed relatively low levels of alcohol, subtle but permanent brain impairment may be seen in her offspring in the form of decreased IQ scores.[43]

Although many other solvents are used widely in industry—for example, in dry cleaning, nail polish removers, spot cleaners, paint thinners, and detergents—there has been very little research on their toxic effects. Nonetheless, there are case reports of mothers who inhaled toluene (while sniffing glue) whose children had abnormally low scores on developmental tests and delayed development of speech and motor function.[44]

Pesticides

More than 600 organophosphate-based pesticides, including insecticides, fungicides, and rodenticides, are registered for use. In the United States alone, about 500 million kilograms of pesticides are applied annually. Although the neurotoxic effects of intense occupational exposure is well established,[45] its impact on the developing brain was only recently confirmed through anthropological research on Yaqui children in Mexico aged four to five.[46] Children with high exposure to a mix of pesticides, including organophosphates, had diminished short-term memory, hand-eye coordination, and drawing ability, whereas unexposed children of the same tribe showed normal development. Likewise, preschool children from agricultural communities in the United States showed poorer performance on motor speed and latency than did those of urban communities.[47] Ecuadoran schoolchildren whose mothers had been exposed to organophosphates and other pesticides, from working in greenhouses during pregnancy, showed visuospatial deficits compared with their unexposed peers.[48] Several other studies have shown that both prenatal and postnatal exposure to pesticides is associated with delays in children's simple reaction time, persistent problems with short-term memory and attention span, decreases in head circumference and birth weight, and slowing of reflexes.[49] Although organophosphates in pesticides can undoubtedly cause developmental neurotoxicity, the data are insufficient to determine the potential hazard to the developing brain posed by individual compounds among the dozens of organophosphates in use worldwide.

EMERGING NEUROTOXIC SUBSTANCES

Although minimal research has been conducted to date on the substances discussed in this section, preliminary research indicates an urgent need for follow-up research on the toxic effects of these substances on the developing brain.

Manganese

Manganese neurotoxicity has been well documented in adults who come into contact with it at work. Parkinsonism is typically found in adults who have been overexposed to manganese.[50] It is urgent that researchers examine the impact of manganese on children's developing brains: the organic manganese compound methylcyclopentadienyl manganese tricarbonyl has been added to gasoline in Australia and Canada and may be used in the United States and other countries in the near future. Manganese is also sometimes found in drinking water. In a study of 247 newborns in Paris, France, high manganese concentrations in umbilical cord blood were associated with impaired neurobehavioral development at age nine months.[51] Exposure to manganese following an explosion at a toxic waste site in the United States and from contaminated drinking water in Bangladesh have also been associated with neurological impairment in children.[52]

Fluoride

Although fluoride has not yet been proven to be toxic to adults, three studies conducted in China have revealed a link between exposure to fluoride and developmental abnormalities. In two studies, children aged eight to thirteen who had been exposed to high concentrations of naturally occurring fluoride in their drinking water had significantly lower IQs compared with a control group of children.[53] A third study, which involved 477 children from twenty-two Chinese villages, suggested that even low concentrations of water fluoride exposure were associated with IQ deficits, compared with children exposed to normal concentrations (below 1 mg/L).[54]

Perchlorate

Perchlorate is a widespread contaminant of groundwater in the United States caused by ammonium perchlorate used as a solid-fuel propellant for rockets and missiles.[55] Although perchlorate exposure does not damage the brain, it is damaging to the thyroid gland. If pregnant women have impaired thyroid function as a result of perchlorate exposure, their thyroid dysfunction can in turn have damaging effects on the developing brain of their fetus.[56] But to date, drinking water standards for perchlorate are set at levels to protect adults, and do not include child-protective safety factors.

A PANDEMIC OF DEVELOPMENTAL NEUROTOXICITY BENEATH THE RADAR SCREEN

Among the five substances that have been definitively shown to damage children's developing brains—lead, methylmercury, PCBs, arsenic, and toluene—the paths that led to their discovery have been remarkably similar. First, adult neurotoxicity was established following exposure at the workplace; second, children who were accidentally poisoned by high doses exhibited subsequent brain damage; and third, it was discovered that children who had been exposed to these substances prenatally *at doses that are not toxic to adults* exhibited neurobehavioral deficits ranging from lower IQs to emotional abnormalities. In other words, in all five cases, after adult neurotoxicity was established, it was discovered that children are neurologically vulnerable to lower exposures and that the damage to their developing brains is more pervasive. And so this leads us to feel great concern about the 196 other chemicals that have been proven to be toxic to the adult brain but whose effects in children have not been studied.

The 201 chemicals known to be neurotoxic to humans are listed at the end of this chapter. Although these chemicals may well have caused impaired brain development in millions of children worldwide, the impact of these exposures is not apparent from available health statistics. But beyond these few hundred chemicals, the impact on the human brain of approximately 80,000 industrial chemicals that are currently in use have not been adequately tested. The combined evidence suggests that neurodevelopmental disorders caused by industrial chemicals have created a silent pandemic in modern society.

The well-documented effects of lead exposure—lowered IQ, shortened attention span, increased impulsivity, heightened aggressiveness, slowed motor coordination, and impaired memory and language skills—is an object lesson on the critical importance of (1) examining the role of all 201 known neurotoxins to which children are routinely exposed in isolation and in combination; and (2) evaluating them as risk factors in the development of psychological disturbances. Virtually every child in the world is at risk for exposure to neurotoxic industrial chemicals. Those in wealthy nations are close to the by-products of multiple industries, and those in poor nations are exposed to poisons such as the highly dangerous pesticides that have been banned in the United States but are exported to developing nations where environmental and occupational standards are often weak or poorly enforced.[57]

PREVENTION

A pandemic of neurodevelopmental toxicity caused by industrial chemicals is, in theory, preventable. Testing new chemicals before they are allowed to be marketed is a highly efficient means of preventing toxicity, but testing has not been required until recent years. Of the thousands of chemicals used commercially, fewer than half have been subjected to even token laboratory testing for toxicity.[58] Nearly 3,000 of these substances are produced in quantities of almost 500,000 kg every year, but for nearly half these high-volume chemicals, no basic toxicity data are publicly available, and for 80 percent of them, there is no information about developmental or pediatric toxicity.[59]

In the United States a legal mandate to require testing of new industrial chemicals was established in the Toxic Substance Control Act in 1977, but it is largely unenforced.[60] And when new chemicals are tested, access to the data is often restricted to avoid breaching the confidentiality of the business that produces the chemical. More extensive chemical testing is taking place in the European Union, through its program for the Registration, Evaluation, and Authorisation of Chemicals, known as REACH. However, the proposed legislation does not require testing the impact of the chemicals on children, whose rapid neurological development renders them much more vulnerable and vulnerable at lower levels of exposure. And neither the testing protocols in the United States nor in the European Union include neurobehavioral measures such as IQ, mood disturbances, attention span, or impulse control. Current protocols rely mainly on crude indices, such as brain weight and gross morphology.[61] The great danger in this limited protocol is that crude measures may miss significant impairments and falsely negate the need for regulation or intervention. And yet a rigorous protocol for assessing developmental neurotoxicity has already been developed by the Organization for Economic Cooperation and Development (OECD) in 1999.[62]

The number of chemicals that have been proven to cause neurotoxicity in laboratory studies probably exceeds 1,000[63]—far more than the 201 that have been documented as neurotoxic to humans. Despite the absence of systematic testing, in light of what we know about the physiology of brain development, there is high probability that many of these 1,000 are toxic to the developing brain. And so the few substances that *have* been tested are merely the tip of the iceberg.

Large-scale prospective epidemiological studies now being conducted in Europe[64] and the National Children's Study in the United States will be especially informative about the relationship between early exposures and neurodevelopmental disorders. When the results of these investigations are pooled internationally, they will provide dose–response associations that can guide future efforts in disease prevention. The substances listed at the end of this chapter—especially those most prevalent in food, drinking water, and the environment—will be given special attention in the National Children's Study. But even in the best-case scenario—wide-scale testing of all 201 known neurotoxins for their dose-related impact on children's developing brains—it could take decades for the results to be confirmed, and millions of children will continue to be needlessly exposed to industrial chemicals known to harm the human brain.

The U.S. Food Quality Protection Act requires pesticide standards to be set at levels that protect not only adults but also infants against developmental toxicity. If these levels have not yet been assessed through research, the Act requires that safety levels for infants be estimated on the basis of what is known to be safe for adults. However, application of this requirement has been uneven at best because regulatory authorities are not always aware of the extreme vulnerability of the prenatal and infant brain.

As with pesticides, all established neurotoxins to which pregnant women and young children are routinely exposed should be set at values that take into account the unique sensitivity of pregnant women and young children, with a view to protecting brain development. If such a precautionary approach were implemented, as recently undertaken in the European Union, then early indications of the potential for a serious toxic effect (e.g., developmental neurotoxicity) would lead to strict regulation that could later be relaxed if and when subsequent documentation showed less harm resulting than anticipated.[65] Children's health practitioners should become well versed in the literature on neurotoxic industrial chemicals to be able to counsel their patients, especially pregnant mothers, about the importance of avoiding exposure to chemicals of unknown and untested neurotoxic potential.

CHEMICALS (N = 201) KNOWN TO BE TOXIC TO THE ADULT HUMAN

Metals and Inorganic Compounds

Aluminum compounds	Azide compounds	Carbon monoxide
Arsenic and arsenic compounds*	Barium compounds	Cyanide compounds
	Bismuth compounds	Decaborane

Diborane
Ethylmercury
Fluoride compounds
Hydrogen sulphide
Lead and lead
    compounds*
Lithium compounds

Manganese and
    manganese
    compounds
Mercury and mercuric
    compounds
Methylmercury*
Nickel carbonyl

Pentaborane
Phosphine
Phosphorus
Selenium compounds
Tellurium compounds
Thallium compounds
Tin compounds

Organic Solvents

Acetone
Benzene
Benzyl alcohol
Carbon disulphide
Chloroform
Chloroprene
Cumene
Cyclohexane
Cyclohexanol
Cyclohexanone
Dibromochloropropane
Dichloroacetic acid
1,3-Dichloropropene
Diethylene glycol
N,N-Dimethyl-
    formamide

2-Ethoxyethyl acetate
Ethyl acetate
Ethylene dibromide
Ethylene glycol
n-Hexane
Isobutyronitrile
Isophorone
Isopropyl alcohol
Isopropylacetone
Methanol
Methyl butyl ketone
Methyl cellosolve
Methyl ethyl ketone
Methylcyclopentane
Methylene chloride
Nitrobenzene

2-Nitropropane
1-Pentanol
Propyl bromide
Pyridine   .
Styrene
Tetrachloroethane
Tetrachloroethylene
Toluene*
1,1,1-Trichloroethane
Trichloroethylene
Vinyl chloride
Xylene

Other Organic Substances

Acetone cyanohydrin
Acrylamide
Acrylonitrile
Allyl chloride
Aniline
1,2-Benzenedicarboni-
    trile
Benzonitrile
Butylated triphenyl
    phosphate
Caprolactam
Cyclonite

Dibutyl phthalate
3-(Dimethylamino)-
    propanenitrile
Diethylene glycol
    diacrylate
Dimethyl sulphate
Dimethylhydrazine
Dinitrobenzene
Dinitrotoluene
Ethylbis(2-
    chloroethyl)amine
Ethylene

Ethylene oxide
Fluoroacetamide
Fluoroacetic acid
Hexachlorophene
Hydrazine
Hydroquinone
Methyl chloride
Methyl formate
Methyl iodide
Methyl methacrylate
p-Nitroaniline
Phenol

p-Phenylenediamine
Phenylhydrazine
Polybrominated
  biphenyl
Polybrominated
  diphenyl ethers

Polychlorinated
  biphenyls*
Propylene oxide
TCDD
Tributyl phosphate

2,2′,2″-Trichlorotriethy-
  lamine
Trimethyl phosphate
Tri-o-tolyl phosphate
Triphenyl phosphate

Pesticides

Aldicarb
Aldrin
Bensulide
Bromophos
Carbaryl
Carbofuran
Carbophenothion
α-Chloralose
Chlordane
Chlordecone
Chlorfenvinphos
Chlormephos
Chlorpyrifos
Chlorthion
Coumaphos
Cyhalothrin
Cypermethrin
2,4-D
DDT
Deltamethrin
Demeton
Dialifor
Diazinon
Dichlofenthion
Dichlorvos
Dieldrin
Dimefox
Dimethoate
Dinitrocresol
Dinoseb

Dioxathion
Disulphoton
Edifenphos
Endosulphan
Endothion
Endrin
EPN
Ethiofencarb
Ethion
Ethoprop
Fenitrothion
Fensulphothion
Fenthion
Fenvalerate
Fonofos
Formothion
Heptachlor
Heptenophos
Hexachlorobenzene
Isobenzan
Isolan
Isoxathion
Leptophos
Lindane
Merphos
Metaldehyde
Methamidophos
Methidathion
Methomyl
Methyl bromide

Methyl demeton
Methyl parathion
Mevinphos
Mexacarbate
Mipafox
Mirex
Monocrotophos
Naled
Nicotine
Oxydemeton-methyl
Parathion
Pentachlorophenol
Phorate
Phosphamidon
Phospholan
Propaphos
Propoxur
Pyriminil
Sarin
Schradan
Soman
Sulprofos
2,4,5-T
Tebupirimfos
Tefluthrin
Terbufos
Thiram
Toxaphene
Trichlorfon
Trichloronat

---

* Asterisks mark the five chemicals that, in addition to being toxic to the adult human, are documented to cause developmental neurotoxicity.

Series Afterword

The rich diversity of cultures created by humankind is testament to our ability to develop and adapt in diverse ways. But however varied different cultures may be, children are not endlessly malleable—they all share basic psychological and physical needs that must be met to ensure healthy development. The Childhood in America series examines the extent to which American culture meets children's irreducible needs. Without question, many children growing up in the United States lead privileged lives. They have been spared the ravages of war, poverty, malnourishment, sexism, and racism. However, despite our nation's resources, not all children share these privileges. Additionally, values that are central to American culture—such as self-reliance, individualism, privacy of family life, and consumerism—have created a climate in which parenting has become intolerably labor-intensive, and children are being taxed beyond their capacity for healthy adaptation. Record levels of violence, psychiatric disturbance, poverty, apathy, and despair among our children speak to our current cultural crisis.

Although our elected officials profess their commitment to "family values," policies that support family life are woefully lacking and are inferior to those in other industrialized nations. American families are burdened by inadequate parental leave, a health care system that does not provide universal coverage for children, a minimum wage that is not a living wage, "welfare to work" policies that require parents to leave their children for long stretches of time, unregulated and inadequately subsidized day care, an unregulated entertainment industry that exposes children to sex and violence, and a two-tiered public education system that delivers inferior education to poor children and frequently ignores individual differences in learning styles and profiles of intelligence. As a result, many families are taxed to the breaking point. In addition, our fascination with technological innovation is creating a family lifestyle that is dominated by the screen rather than human interaction.

The Childhood in America series seeks out leading childhood experts from across the disciplines to promote dialogue, research, and understanding regarding how best to raise and educate psychologically healthy children and to ensure that they will acquire the wisdom, heart, and courage needed to make choices for the betterment of society.

Sharna Olfman, PhD
Series Editor

Notes

CHAPTER 1

1. Roberts, E. (2007). The childhood bipolar epidemic: Brat or bipolar? In *Bipolar Children: Cutting-Edge Controversy, Insight, and Research*, ed. Sharna Olfman. Westport, CT: Praeger.

2. Healy, D. (2007). Bipolar syndrome by proxy? The case of pediatric bipolar disorder. In *Bipolar Children: Cutting-Edge Controversy, Insight, and Research*, ed. Sharna Olfman. Westport, CT: Praeger.

3. *Journal of the American Academy of Child and Adolescent Psychiatry*, 46, January 1, 2007, 107.

4. Ibid., 114.

5. Ibid., 114.

6. Ibid., 116.

7. Ibid., 115.

8. Burston, D. (2007). An invisible plague: Pediatric bipolar disorder and the chemical colonization of childhood. In *Bipolar Children: Cutting-Edge Controversy, Insight, and Research*, ed. Sharna Olfman. Westport, CT: Praeger.

9. Healy, D. (2007). *See* note 2.

10. Ibid.

11. Ibid.

12. See chapters by Diller, Healy, and Roberts.

13. Healy, D. (2007). *See* note 2.

14. SSRI antidepressants are selective serotonin reuptake inhibitors.

15. Olfman, S. (ed.). (2006). *No Child Left Different*. Westport, CT: Praeger.

16. Bronfenbrenner, U. (1988). Strengthening family systems. In *The Parental Leave Crisis: Toward a National Policy*, eds. E. F. Zigler and M. Frank. New Haven, CT: Yale University Press.

17. Bronfenbrenner, U. (1992). Child care in the Anglo-Saxon mode. In *Child Care in Context*, eds. M. E. Lamb et al. Hillsdale, NJ: Lawrence Erlbaum.

18. Karen, R. (1998). *Becoming Attached: First Relationships and How They Shape Our Capacity to Love*. New York: Oxford University.

19. Gerehardt, S. (2004). *Why Love Matters: How Affection Shapes a Baby's Brain.* New York: Brunner-Routledge.

CHAPTER 2

1. Applbaum, K. (2004). *The Marketing Era*. New York: Routledge.

2. United States Patent 4,988,731. Date of Patent: January 29, 1991; United States Patent 5,212,326. Date of Patent: May 18, 1993.

3. Forty-fourth Psychopharmacologic Drugs Advisory Committee Meeting. (1995, February 6). NDA 20-320: Depakote. Transcript of proceedings. Washington, DC: Department of Health and Human Services.

4. Ghaemi, S. N. (2001). On defining "mood stabilizer." *Bipolar Disorder*, 3, 154–158.

5. Healy, D. (2006). The Latest Mania. Selling Bipolar Disorder. *PLoS Medicine*. Available at http://dx.doi.org/10.1371/journal.pmed.0030185.

6. Goodwin, F. K., and Jamison, K. R. (1990). *Manic-Depressive Illness*. New York: Oxford University Press.

7. Moynihan, R., and Cassels, A. (2005). *Selling Sickness*. New York: Nation Books.

8. Eli Lilly and Company. (2004). *Staying Well . . . with Bipolar Disorder. Relapse Prevention Booklet*. Produced in association with the Manic-Depressive Fellowship of Great Britain, 17.

9. De Hert, M., Thys, E., Magiels, G., et al. (2005). *Anything or Nothing. Self-guide for People with Bipolar Disorder*. Antwerp: Uitgeverij Houtekiet, 35.

10. Joukamaa, M., et al. (2006). Schizophrenia, neuroleptic medication, and mortality. *British Journal of Psychiatry* 188, 122–127.

11. Colton, C. W., and Manderscheid, R.W. (2006). Congruencies in increased mortality rates, years of potential life lost, and causes of death among public mental health clients in eight states. *Preventing Chronic Disease*. Available at http://www.cdc.gov/pcd/issues/2006/apr/05_0180.htm.

12. Healy, D. (2006). *See* note 5; Storosum, J. G., Wohlfarth, T., Gispen de Wied, C. C., et al. (2005). Suicide risk in placebo-controlled trials of treatment for acute manic episode and prevention of manic-depressive episode. *American Journal of Psychiatry*, 162, 799–802.

13. Ernst, C. L., and Goldberg, J. F. (2002). The reproductive safety profile of mood stabilizers, atypical antipsychotics, and broad-spectrum psychotropics. *Journal of Clinical Psychiatry* 63, Supplement 4, 42–55.

14. Healy, D. (2004). *Let Them Eat Prozac*. New York: New York University Press, Chapter 4.

15. Jamison, K. R. (1993). *Touched with Fire. Manic-Depressive Illness and the Artistic Temperament*. New York: Simon & Schuster.

16. Eli Lilly and Company. (2004). *Mood Diary*. Produced in consultation with the Manic-Depressive Fellowship of Great Britain.

17. Astra Zeneca. (2006). www.Isitreallydepression.com.

18. Healy, D. (2002). *The Creation of Psychopharmacology*. Cambridge, MA: Harvard University Press.

19. Child and Adolescent Bipolar Foundation. (2006). http://www.bipolarhelpcenter.com/resources/mdq.jsp.

20. Healy, D. (in press). *Mania*. Baltimore, MD: Johns Hopkins University Press.

21. Papolos, D., and Papolos, J. (2000). *The Bipolar Child*. New York: Random House, 14.

22. Isaac, G. (2001). *Bipolar Not ADHD. Unrecognized Epidemic of Manic-Depressive Illness in Children*. Lincoln, NE: Writers' Club Press.

23. Findling, R. L., Kowatch, R. A., and Post, R. M. (2003). *Pediatric Bipolar Disorder. A Handbook for Clinicians*. London: Martin Dunitz.

24. Hebert, B. (2005). *My Bipolar Roller Coaster Feeling Book*. Victoria, BC: Trafford Publishing.

25. Anglada, T. (2004). *Brandon and the Bipolar Bear*. Victoria, BC: Trafford Publishing.

26. Brooks, K. (2000, July 19). No small burden. Families with mentally ill children confront health care shortcomings, undeserved stigma of "bad parenting." Dallas: Star-Telegram.

27. Kluger, J., and Song, S. (2002, August 19). Young and bipolar. Once called manic depression, the disorder afflicted adults. Now it's striking kids. Why? *Time* magazine, 30–41.

28. Volkmar, F. R. (2002). Changing perspectives on mood disorders in children. *American Journal of Psychiatry*, 159, 893–894.

29. Juvenile Bipolar Research Foundation. (2005). www.jbrf.org/cbq/cbq_survey.cfm.

30. Ibid.

31. Baethge, C., Glovinsky, R., and Baldessarini, R. J. (2004). Manic-depressive illness in children: An early twentieth century view by Theodore Ziehen (1862–1950). *History of Psychiatry*, 15, 201–226.

32. Kyte, Z. A., Carlsson, G. A., and Goodyer, I. M. (2006). Clinical and neuropsychological characteristics of child and adolescent bipolar disorder. *Psychological Medicine*, 36, 1197–1211.

33. Geller, B., et al. (1996). *Washington University in St Louis Kiddie Schedule for Affective Disorders and Schizophrenia (Wash-U-KSADS)*. St Louis: Washington University.

34. Geller, B., et al. (2003). Phenomenology and longitudinal course of children with a prepubertal and early adolescent bipolar disorder phenotype. In Geller, B., DelBello, M. P. (eds.). *Bipolar Disorder in Childhood and Early Adolescence*. New York: The Guilford Press, 25–50.

35. Faraone, S. V., et al. (1997). Attention-deficit/hyperactivity disorder with bipolar disorder: A familial subtype? *Journal of the American Academy of Child and Adolescent Psychiatry*, 36, 1378–1387.

36. Lewinsohn, P., Klein, D., and Seeley, J. (2000). Bipolar disorder during adolescence and young adulthood in a community sample. *Bipolar Disorder*, 2, 281–293.

37. National Institute of Mental Health. (2001). Research Roundtable on Prepubertal Bipolar Disorder. *Journal of the American Academy of Child and Adolescent Psychiatry*, 40, 871–878.

38. Juvenile Bipolar Research Foundation. (2005). www.jbrf.org/juv_bipolar/faq.html.

39. Kowatch, R. A., et al., and the Child Psychiatric Workgroup on Bipolar Disorder. (2005). Treatment guidelines for children and adolescents with bipolar disorder. *Journal of the American Academy of Child and Adolescent Psychiatry*, 44, 213–235.

40. Harris, J. (2005). The increased diagnosis of juvenile "bipolar disorder," what are we treating? *Psychiatric Services*, 56, 529–531.

41. Dilsaver, S. (2005). Review of J. Harris. *Journal of Bipolar Disorders*, 4, 8.

42. Mick, E., et al. (2004). Comparative efficacy of atypical antipsychotics for pediatric bipolar disorder. *Acta psychiatrica Scandinavica*, 1110, 50, 29; Mick, E., et al. (2004). Open trial of atypical antipsychotics in preschoolers with bipolar disorder. *Acta psychiatrica Scandinavica*, 1110, 51, 29.

43. Cooper, W., et al. (2006). Trends in prescribing of antipsychotic medications for U.S. children. *Ambulatory Pediatrics*, 6, 79–83.

44. Post, R. M. (2002, October 17). Treatment resistance in bipolar disorder. Presented to the October 17, 2002 Meeting of the Royal College of Psychiatrists at Newcastle, England.

45. Harris, M., Chandran, S., Chakroborty, N., et al. (2005). Service utilization in bipolar disorders, 1890 and 1990 compared. *History of Psychiatry*, 16, 423–434.

CHAPTER 3

1. Wozniak J., et al. (1995). Mania-like symptoms suggestive of childhood-onset bipolar disorder in clinically referred children. *Journal of the Academy of Child and Adolescent Psychiatry*, 34, 867–876.

2. Biederman J. (August 1996). Are stimulants overprescribed for children with behavioral problems? *Pediatric News*, 26.

3. Castle L., et al. (2007). Trends in medication treatment for ADHD. *Journal of Attention Disorders*, 10, 335–342.

4. Pelletier, G., Geoffroy, G., and Robaey, P. (1996). Mania in children (letter). *Journal of the American Academy of Child and Adolescent Psychiatry*, 35, 1257–1258.

5. Geller, B., and Luby, J. (1997). Child and adolescent bipolar disorder: A review of the past 10 years. *Journal of the American Academy of Child and Adolescent Psychiatry*, 36, 1168–1177.

6. American Psychiatric Association. *Diagnostic and Statistical Manual of Mental Disorders, Third Edition*. (1980). Washington, DC: American Psychiatric Association.

7. Rutter, M. (1983). Behavioral studies: Questions and finds on the concept of a distinctive syndrome. In *Developmental Neuropsychiatry*, ed. M. Rutter. New York: Guilford Press, 273–274.

8. Kirk, S. A., and Kutchins, H. (1992). *The Selling of DSM: The Rhetoric of Science in Psychiatry*. New York: Aldine De Gruyter.

9. Carlson, G. A., et al. (1992). The effects of methylphenidate and lithium on attention and activity level. *Journal of the American Academy of Child and Adolescent Psychiatry*, 31, 262–270.

10. Kramer, P. (1993). *Listening to Prozac*. New York: Viking Penguin, 32–33.

11. Pam, A. (1995). Biological psychiatry: Science or pseudoscience? In *Pseudoscience in Biological Psychiatry*, eds. C. A. Ross and A. Pam. New York: John Wiley, 7–35.

12. Biederman, J., on the *NBC Nightly News*, May 1996.

13. Biederman won the prestigious Rieger Prize for child psychiatric research in the early 1990s.

14. Schwartz, J. M., et al. (1996). Systematic changes in cerebral glucose metabolic rate after successful behavior modification treatment of obsessive-compulsive disorder. *Archives of General Psychiatry* 54, 109–113.

15. In 1995 I attended a three-day psychopharmacology conference hosted by the Biederman team in Boston. As part of the conference I had an opportunity to discuss at length an adolescent's case with Thomas Spencer, one of the members of the Harvard psychopharmacology clinic. Spencer's insistent repeated focus on the neuropsychiatric aspects of this boy's history in spite of multiple family and gender identification issues gave me a sense of reverse *déjà vu* regarding some of the discussions I used to have with the faculty from Columbia's highly traditional psychoanalytic New York State Psychiatric Institute in the mid-1970s when I was a medical student.

16. A list of Biederman's financial associations with the pharmaceutical industry at the end of medical journal articles typically occupies a quarter-column of the page.

17. A relatively "unknown" adult psychiatrist received nearly $700,000 in 2006 from the drug industry in Minnesota, according to an article by Gardiner Harris in the *New York Times* (Prescription for influence: Beyond the label: Psychiatrists, troubled children and the drug industry's role, May 10, 2007, p. 1). The drug industry's payments to Biederman and his group, given their prominence, can only be presumed to run into the millions.

18. Brennan, T. A., et al. (2006). Health industry practices that create conflicts of interest: A policy proposal for academic medical centers. *Journal of the American Medical Association*, 295, 429–433.

19. Bhandari, M., et al. (2004). Association between industry funding and statistically significant pro-industry findings in medical and surgical randomized trials. *Canadian Medical Association Journal*, 170, 477–480.

20. An example was the drug industry–supported mass mailing of a meta-analysis on the supposed protective effects of stimulant medication against later drug abuse by Tim Wilens and Joseph Biederman in 2003. The mailing was sent to every pediatrician and child psychiatrist in the country.

21. Breggin, P. (2001). *Talking Back to Ritalin*. Cambridge, MA: De Capo.

22. Geller, B. (1997). *See* note 5.

23. American Academy of Child and Adolescent Psychiatry. (2007). Practice parameters for the assessment and treatment of children and adolescents with bipolar disorder. *Journal of the American Academy of Child and Adolescent Psychiatry*, 46, 107–125.

24. Ibid.

25. Papolos, D., and Papolos, J. (2006). *The Bipolar Child: The Definitive and Reassuring Guide to Childhood's Most Misunderstood Disorder*. New York: Broadway.

26. Groopman, J. (2007, April 9). What's normal? The difficulty of diagnosing bipolar disorder in children. *New Yorker*, 28–33.

27. Stubbe, D. E., and Thomas, W. J. (2002). A survey of early-career child and adolescent psychiatrists: Professional activities and perceptions. *Journal of the American Academy of Child and Adolescent Psychiatry*, 41, 123–130.

28. Biederman, J., et al. (2005). Open-label, 8-week trial of olanzapine and risperidone for the treatment of bipolar disorder in preschool-age children. *Biological Psychiatry*, 58, 589–594.

29. American Academy of Child and Adolescent Psychiatry. (2007). *See* note 23.

30. Ibid.

31. Carey, B. (2007, February 27). Debate over children and psychiatric drugs. *New York Times*, 1.

32. Lavoie, D. (2007, March 25). A child dies and psychiatry is scrutinized. *Associated Press*.

CHAPTER 4

1. Bowers, M. (1974). Central dopamine turnover in schizophrenic syndromes. *Archives of General Psychiatry*, 31, 50–54.

2. Post, R., Fink, E., Carpenter, W., et al. (1975). Cerebrospinal fluid amine metabolites in acute schizophrenia. *Archives of General Psychiatry*, 32, 1063–1068.

3. Haracz, J. (1982). The dopamine hypothesis: An overview of studies with schizophrenic patients. *Schizophrenia Bulletin*, 8, 438–458.

4. Lee, T., and Seeman, P. (1978). Binding of ^{3}H-neuroleptics and ^{3}H-apomorphine in schizophrenic brains. *Nature*, 374, 897–900.

5. Burt, D., Creese, I., and Snyder, S. (1977). Antischizophrenic drugs: Chronic treatment elevates dopamine receptor binding in brain. *Science*, 196, 326–328; Mackay, A., et al. (1982). Increased brain dopamine and dopamine receptors in schizophrenia. *Archives of General Psychiatry*, 3, 991–997; Kornhuber, J., et al. (1989). ^{3}H-Siperone binding sites in post-mortem brains from schizophrenic patients: Relationship to neuroleptic drug treatment, abnormal movements, and positive symptoms. *Journal of Neural Transmission*, 75, 1–10. Kornhuber, J., et al. (1989).

6. Kornhuber, J., et al. (1989). *See* note 5.

7. Kane, J., and Freeman, H. (1994). Towards more effective antipsychotic treatment. *British Journal of Psychiatry*, 165, 22–31.

8. White, F. (1983). Differential effects of classical and atypical antipsychotic drugs on A_9 and A_{10} dopamine neurons. *Science*, 221, 1054–1056.

9. Lacasse, J., and Leo, J. (2005). Serotonin and depression: A disconnect between the advertisements and the scientific literature. *PLoS Medicine*, 2, 1211–1216.

10. Ibid.

11. Healy, D. (2005). Ads for SSRI antidepressants are misleading. *PloS Medicine* news release, November 2005.

12. Jacobs, B. (1991). Serotonin and behavior: Emphasis on motor control. *Journal of Clinical Psychiatry*, 52 (12 Suppl), 151–162.

13. Lacasse and Leo (2005). *See* note 9.

14. Hyman, S., and Nestler, E. (1996). Initiation and adaptation: A paradigm for understanding psychotropic drug action. *American Journal of Psychiatry*, 153, 151–161.

15. Ibid.

16. Torrey, E. (2001). *The Invisible Plague: The Rise of Mental Illness from 1750 to the Present.* New Brunswick, NJ: Rutgers University Press, 315.

17. The calculation for the number of disabled mentally ill is as follows: In 1987 there were 800,139 SSDI recipients who were disabled because of mental illness. There were 2,630,999 SSI recipients diagnosed as mentally ill. One out of every eight recipients of SSDI—100,017 people—also received an SSI payment. Thus, the number of disabled mentally ill in 1987 is: 800,139 1 2,630,999 2 100,017 5 3,331,120. The same formula was applied to calculate the number of disabled mentally ill in 2004.

18. Bradley, C. In Lewis, N., and Pacella B., eds. (1945). *Modern Trends in Child Psychiatry.* New York: International Universities Press, 135–154.

19. Lurie, L., and Lurie, M. Psychoses in children. *Journal of Pediatrics,* 36, 801–809.

20. Barton Hall, M. (1952). Our present knowledge about manic-depressive states in childhood. *Child's Nervous System,* 9, 319–325.

21. Anthony, E., and Scott, P. (1960). Manic-depressive psychosis in childhood. *Journal of Child Psychology and Psychiatry,* 1, 53–72.

22. Weinberg, W., and Brumback, R. (1976). Mania in childhood, case studies and literature review. *American Journal of Disease in Childhood,* 130, 380–385.

23. DeLong, G. (1978). Lithium carbonate treatment of select behavior disorders in children suggesting manic-depressive illness. *Journal of Pediatrics,* 93, 689–694.

24. Davis, R. (1979). Manic-depressive variant syndrome of childhood. *American Journal of Psychiatry,* 136, 702–706.

25. Lewinsohn, P., Klein, D., and Seeley, J. (1995). Bipolar disorders in a community sample of older adolescents. *Journal of the American Academy of Child and Adolescent Psychiatry,* 34, 454–463.

26. Faedda, G., Baldessarini, R., Suppes, T., et al. (1995). Pediatric-onset bipolar disorder. *Harvard Review of Psychiatry,* 3, 171–195.

27. Papolos, D., and Papolos, J. (2000). *The Bipolar Child.* New York: Broadway.

28. Kluger, J., and Song, S. (2002, August 19). Young and bipolar. *Time* magazine.

29. Diller, L. (1996). The run on Ritalin. *The Hastings Center Report,* 26, 12–18.

30. Drug Enforcement Administration. (1995). "Methylphenidate: A Background Paper." Washington, DC: U.S. Department of Justice.

31. Ibid.

32. Volkow, N., Ding, Y., Fowler, J., et al. (1995). Is methylphenidate like cocaine? Studies on their pharmacokinetics and distribution in the human brain. *Archives of General Psychiatry,* 52, 456–463.

33. Drug Enforcement Administration. (1995). *See* note 30; Breggin, P. (1999). Psychostimulants in the treatment of children diagnosed with ADHD. *International Journal of Risk and Safety in Medicine,* 12, 3–35.

34. Researchers had identified amphetamine-induced psychosis as a problem in the 1950s. Moreover, psychiatric researchers during the 1970s and 1980s used methylphenidate to deliberately exacerbate psychotic symptoms in schizophrenic patients. These experiments were conducted to investigate the hypothesis that dopamine overactivity in the brain was the cause of schizophrenia. Although the researchers did not find that people diagnosed with schizophrenia had overactive dopamine systems, their research did show that dopamine-releasing drugs had the potential to trigger psychosis.

35. National Institute of Mental Health (2000). Child and adolescent bipolar disorder. Available at http://www.nimh.nih.gov/publicat/biopolarupdate.htm.

36. Chandler, J. (2007). Bipolar affective disorder in children and adolescents. Available at http://www.klis.com/chandler/pamphlet/bipolar/bipolar pamphlet.htm.

37. National Alliance for the Mentally Ill. (2001). Facts about childhood-onset bipolar disorder. Available at http://www.healthieryou.com/bipolarch.html.

38. Kluger, J., and Song, S. (2002). See note 28.

39. Biederman, J., Faraone, S., Mick, E., et al. (1996). Attention-deficit hyperactivity disorder and juvenile mania. *Journal of the American Academy of Child and Adolescent Psychiatry, 35*, 997–1008.

40. Reichart, C., Nolen, W., Wals, M., et al. (2002). Bipolar disorder in children and adolescents: A clinical reality? *Acta Neuropsychiatrica, 12*, 132–135. Also see abstracts presented at the Fourth International Conference on Bipolar Disorder, hosted by the Western Psychiatric Institute in Pittsburgh, June 2001.

41. Delate, T., Gelenberg, A., Simmons, V., at al. (2004). Trends in the use of antidepressants in a national sample of commercially insured pediatric patients, 1998–2002. *Psychiatric Services, 55*, 387–391.

42. Moore, T. (1997, December). Hard to swallow. *Washingtonian*, 68–71, 140–145.

43. Breggin, P. (2003). Suicidality, violence and mania caused by selective serotonin reuptake inhibitors (SSRIs): A review and analysis. *International Journal of Risk and Safety in Medicine, 16*, 31–49.

44. Howland, R. (1996). Induction of mania with serotonin reuptake inhibitors. *Journal of Clinical Psychopharmacology, 16*, 425–427.

45. Breggin, P. (2003). See note 42.

46. Bourguignon, R. (1997). Dangers of fluoxetine. *Lancet, 394*, 214.

47. Jain, J., et al. (1992). Fluoxetine in children and adolescents with mood disorders. *Journal of Child and Adolescent Psychopharmacology, 2*, 259–265.

48. Breggin, P. (2003). See note 42.

49. Ibid.

50. Harris, G. (2004, September 14). FDA links drugs to being suicidal. *New York Times*, 1.

51. Faedda, G., et al. (1995). See note 26.

52. McClellan, J., and Werry, J. (1997). Practice parameters for the assessment and treatment of children and adolescents with bipolar disorder. *Journal of the American Academy of Child and Adolescent Psychiatry, 36*, 138–157.

53. Hellander, M., and Burke, T. (1999). Children with bipolar disorder. *Journal of the American Academy of Child and Adolescent Psychiatry, 38*, 495.

54. Bhangoo, R., Lowe, C., and Myers, F. (2003). Medication use in children and adolescents treated in the community for bipolar disorder. *Journal of Child and Adolescent Psychopharmacology, 13*, 515–522.

55. Lansford, A. (2004). Bipolar disorder in childhood and adolescence. http://www.dbpeds.org.

56. Chandler, J. (2007). See note 35.

57. Olfson, M., Blanco, C., Liu, L., et al. (2006). National trends in the outpatient treatment of children and adolescents with antipsychotic drugs. *Archives of General Psychiatry, 63*, 679–685.

CHAPTER 5

1. Acocella, J. (1999). *Creating Hysteria: Women and Multiple Personality Disorder.* Hoboken: Jossey-Bass Publishers.

2. Woodworth, T., Deputy Director, Office of Diversion Control, Drug Enforcement Administration. (2000, May 16). DEA Congressional testimony. Available at http://www.usdoj.gov/dea/pubs/cngrtest/ct051600.htm.

3. Nissen, S. (2006, February 16). Cleveland Clinic interview on the *Diane Rehm Show,* National Public Radio and American University Radio, WAMU 88.5. Washington, DC.

4. Olfson, M., et al. (2006). Number of children and teens treated with antipsychotics increases sharply. *Archives of General Psychiatry, 63,* 679–685.

5. Tanner, L. (2006, March 16). More kids are getting anti-psychotic drugs. Associated Press, Chicago. Available at Web site for the Alliance for Human Research Protection: http://www.ahrp.org/cms/content/view/112/28.

6. Zito, J. M., Safer, D. J., Dos Reis, S., et al. (2003). Psychotropic practice patterns for youth: A 10-year perspective. *Archives of Pediatrics and Adolescent Medicine, 157,* 17–25.

7. Pastor, P. N., and Reuben, C. A. (2002). Attention deficit disorder and learning disability: United States, 1997–98. *Vital and Health Statistics, National Center for Health Statistics,* 10, 206; Kelleher, K. J., McInerny, T. K., Gardner, W. P., et al. (2000). Increasing identification of psychosocial problems: 1979–1996. *Pediatrics* 105, 6, 1320.

8. Matthews, A. W. (2004, August 5). FDA revisits issue of antidepressants for youths. *Wall Street Journal.*

9. WCVB TV-5, ABC Television. (2007, February 7). Available at http://www.thebostonchannel.com/news/10955712/detail.html.

10. Mahoney, S. (2007, March). The brat pack: They interrupt, demand, sulk, scream and talk back. Why are kids today ruder than ever? *Parents,* 122–126.

11. Roberts, E. (2006, October 8). A rush to medicate young minds. *Washington Post.* Available at www.washingtonpost.com/wp-dyn/content/article/2006/10/06/AR2006100601391.

12. Roberts, E. (2006). *Should You Medicate Your Child's Mind? A Child Psychiatrist Makes Sense of Whether to Give Kids Psychiatric Medications.* New York: Marlowe & Co., 25.

13. Waters, R. (2006, January/February). Children in crisis? Concerns about the growing popularity of the bipolar diagnosis. *Psychotherapy Networker.*

14. Roberts, E. (2006). *See* note 12, 32–33.

15. McClellan, J., Kowatch, R., Findling, R., et al. (2006, October). Practice parameters for the assessment and treatment of children and adolescents with bipolar disorder. Unpublished presentation to 53rd Annual Meeting of the American Academy of Child and Adolescent Psychiatry.

16. Roberts, E. (2006). See note 12, 5.

17. Ibid., 43.

18. Ibid., 42.

19. Ibid., 5–6.

20. Ibid., 87–88.

21. Gleason, M. M., and Doctoroff, G. (2006, September). Infant psychiatry. *Psychiatric Times,* 23, 10, 38.

22. Hockridge, Stephanie. (2007, February 28). WCAV TV-19 CBS News. Dangerous diagnoses. Available at http://www.charlottesvillenewsplex.tv/news/headlines/6177266.html.

23. KOTV.com. The News on 6. (2007, March 23). Massachusetts girl's fatal overdose raises questions about psychiatric meds for children. Available at http://www.kotv.com/news/national/story/?id5123325.

24. WCVB TV-5 ABC Television Web site (2007, February 5–7, March 5). Available at http://www.thebostonchannel.com/news/10955712/detail.html.

25. KOTV.com. The News on 6. (2007, March 23). *See* note 23.

26. Roberts, E. (2006). *See* note 12, 46.

CHAPTER 7

1. Halfon, N., McLear, K. T., Schuster, M. A. (eds.). (2002). *Child Rearing in America*. London: Cambridge University Press.

2. Findling, R. L., et al. (2005). Toward an evidenced-based assessment of pediatric bipolar disorder. *Journal of Clinical, Child and Adolescent Psychology*, 34 (3), 433–448; Burston, D. (2006). Diagnosis, drugs, and bipolar disorder in children. In *No Child Left Different*, ed. S. Olfman. Westport, CT: Praeger.

CHAPTER 8

1. Erikson, E. (1956). The problem of ego identity. *Journal of the American Psychoanalytic Association*, 4, 56–121; Erikson, E. (1950). *Childhood and Society*. New York: W.W. Norton.

2. Burston, D. (2007). *Erik Erikson and the American Psyche*. New York: Jason Aronson.

3. Shapiro, E. F., and Fromm, G. (1999). "Erik Erikson's clinical theory." In *Comprehensive Textbook of Psychiatry*, eds. B. J. Sadock and H. I. Kaplan. New York: Williams and Wilkins.

4. Kirk, S., and Kutchins, H. (1997). *Making Us Crazy: The Psychiatric Bible and the Creation of Mental Disorders*. Hawthorne, NY: Aldine de Grutyer; Marius, R. (1999). *Martin Luther: The Christian Between God & Death*. Cambridge, MA: Belknap Press of the Harvard University Press; Kirk, S., and Kutchins, H. (1992). *The Selling of the DSM: The Rhetoric of Science in Psychiatry*. Hawthorne, NY: Aldine de Grutyer.

5. Kirk, S., and Kutchins, H. (1992). *See* note 4.

6. Spiegel, A. (2005, January 3). The dictionary of disorder: How one man revolutionized psychiatry. *New Yorker*, 56–66.

7. Mohr, W. K. (2001). Bipolar disorder in children. *Journal of Psychosocial Nursing and Mental Health Services*, 39(3), 12–23; Biederman, J. (2003). Pediatric bipolar disorder coming of age. *Biological Psychiatry*, 53(11), 931–934; Wozniak, J. (2003). Pediatric bipolar disorder: The new perspective on severe mood dysfunction in children. *Journal of Child and Adolescent Psychopharmacology*, 13(4), 441–451.

8. Kowatch, R. A., et al. (2005). Treatment guidelines for children and adolescents with bipolar disorder. *Journal of the American Academy of Child and Adolescent Psychiatry*, 43(3), 213–235.

9. Lewinsohn, P., Seeley, J., and Klein, D. (2003). Bipolar disorder in adolescents: Epidemiology and suicidal behavior. In *Bipolar Disorders in Children*, eds. B. Geller and M. P. DelBello. New York: Guildford Press, 7–24.

10. Kowatch, R. A., et al. (2005). *See* note 8.

11. McLellan, J. (2005, March). Editorial. *Journal of the American Academy of Child and Adolescent Psychiatry*, 44, 236–239.

12. Kowatch, R. A., et al. (2005). *See* note 8.

13. Knopf, A. (2005). Polypharmacy: New data evaluate prescribing patterns in children and adolescents. *The Brown University Child & Adolescent Psychopharmacology Update*, 7(4), 1, 5–7; Vitiello, B. (2005). Pharmcoepidemiology and pediatric psychopharmacological research. *Journal of Child and Adolescent Psychopharmacology*, 15(1), 10–11; Zito, J. M. S. (2005). Recent child pharmacoepidemiological findings. *Journal of Child and Adolescent Psychopharmacology*, 15(1), 5–9.

14. Sinaikin, P. (2004, February). How I learned to stop worrying and love the *DSM*. *Psychiatric Times*, 103–105.

15. Goffman, I. (1961). *Asylums*. Chicago: University of Chicago Press; Scheff, T. (1966). *Being Mentally Ill: A Sociological Theory*. Chicago: Aldine.

16. Treacher, A., and Baruch, G. (1980). Towards a critical history of the psychiatric profession. In *Critical Psychiatry: The Politics of Mental Health*, ed. D. Ingleby. New York: Pantheon Books.

17. Karen, R. (1998). *Becoming Attached: First Relationships and How They Shape Our Capacity to Love*. New York: Oxford University Press; Greenspan, S. L. (1999). *Building Healthy Minds*. New York: Da Capo Press; Schore, A. (2003). *Affect Regulation and the Repair of the Self*. New York: W.W. Norton; Gerhardt, S. (2004). *Why Love Matters: How Affection Shapes a Baby's Brain*. New York: Brunner-Routledge.

18. Hewlett, S., et al. (1998). *The War against Parents: What We Can Do for America's Beleaguered Moms and Dads*. New York: Houghton Mifflin Co.

19. Burstyn, V. (2005). Techno environmental assaults on children's health. In *Childhood Lost: How American Culture Is Failing Our Kids*, ed. S. Olfman. Westport, CT: Praeger.

20. Olfman, S., ed. (2003). *All Work and No Play: How Educational Reforms Are Harming Our Preschoolers*. Childhood in America, ed. S. Olfman. Westport, CT: Praeger.

21. De Gaetano, G. (2004). *Parenting Well in a Media Age: Keeping Our Kids Human*. Fawnskin, CA: Personhood Press.

22. Breggin, P. (1999). *Reclaiming Our Children: A Healing Plan for a Nation in Crisis*. Cambridge, MA: Perseus Books.

23. Burston, D. (2000). *The Crucible of Experience: R. D. Laing and the Crisis of Psychotherapy*. Cambridge, MA: Harvard University Press.

24. Cohen, D. (1997). Psychoiatrogenics: Introducing chlorapromazine in psychiatry. *Review of Existential Psychology and Psychiatry*, 23(1–3), 206–233.

25. Whitaker, R. (2002). *Mad in America: Bad Science, Bad Medicine and the Mistreatment of the Mentally Ill*. New York: Basic Books.

26. Ibid., 226–232.

27. Lenzer, J. (2004, June 19). Bush plans to screen the whole population for mental illness. *British Medical Journal*, 328; Waters, R. (2005, May–June). Medicating Aliah. *Mother Jones*, 50–55, 86–87.

28. Whitaker, R. (2002). *See* note 26; Waters, R. (2005). *See* note 28; Healy, D. (2003). *Let Them Eat Prozac.* Toronto: James Lorimer & Co.

29. Waters, R. (2005). *See* note 28; Healy, D. (2003). *See* note 29; Hughes, C. W., et al. (1999). The Texas Children's Medication Algorithm Project: Report of the Texas Consensus Panel on Medication Treatment of Childhood Major Depressive Disorder. *Journal of the American Academy of Child and Adolescent Psychiatry,* 38, 11.

30. Healey, D. (2003). *See* note 29.

31. Waters, R. (2005). *See* note 28.

32. Hughes, C. W., et al. (1999). *See* note 30.

33. Lenzer, J. (2004). *See* note 28; Waters, R. (2005). *See* note 28; Szasz, T. (2004). Pharmacracy in America. *Society,* (July/August): 54–58.

34. Levine, M. (2002). *A Mind at a Time.* New York: Simon and Schuster.

35. Burstyn, V. (2005). *See* note 20.

36. Kirsner, D. (2000). *Unfree Associations: Inside Psychoanalytic Institutes.* London: Process Press.

CHAPTER 9

1. Boyle, C. A., Decoufle, P., and Yeargin-Allsopp, M. (1994). Prevalence and health impact of developmental disabilities in U.S. children. *Pediatrics,* 93, 399–403.

2. National Research Council. (2000). *Scientific Frontiers in Developmental Toxicology and Risk Assessment.* Washington, DC: National Academy Press.

3. Dobbing, J. (1968). Vulnerable periods in developing brain. In *Applied Neurochemistry,* eds. A. N. Davison and J. Dobbing. Philadelphia: Davis, 287–318.

4. Ibid., 287–316; Rodier, P. M. (1995). Developing brain as a target of toxicity. *Environmental Health Perspectives,* 103 (Suppl. 6), 73–76; Rice, D., and Barone, S., Jr. (2000). Critical periods of vulnerability for the developing nervous system: Evidence from humans and animal models. *Environmental Health Perspectives,* 108 (Suppl. 3), 511–533.

5. Dobbing, J. (1968). 287–316. *See* note 3; Rice, D., and Barone, S., Jr. (2000). *See* note 4.

6. Anderson, H. R., Nielsen, J. B., and Grandjean, P. (2000). Toxicologic evidence of developmental neurotoxicity of environmental chemicals. *Toxicology,* 144, 121–127.

7. Sakamoto, M., et al. (2004). Maternal and fetal mercury and n-3 polyunsaturated fatty acids as a risk and benefit of fish consumption to fetus. *Environmental Science and Technology,* 38, 3860–3863.

8. Adinolfi, M. (1985). The development of the human blood-CSF-brain barrier. *Developmental Medicine and Child Neurology,* 27, 532–537.

9. Rodier, P. M. (1995). *See* note 4; Rice, D., and Barone, S., Jr. (2000). *See* note 4.

10. National Research Council. (1993). *Pesticides in the Diets of Infants and Children.* Washington: National Academy Press; Ginsberg, G., Hattis, D., and Sonawane, B. (2004). Incorporating pharmacokinetic differences between children and adults in assessing children's risks to environmental toxicants. *Toxicology and Applied Pharmacology,* 198, 164–183.

11. Jensen, A. A., and Slorach, S. (eds.). (1991). *Chemical Contaminants in Human Milk.* Boca Raton: CRC Press.

12. Landrigan, P. J. (1989). The toxicity of lead at low dose. *British Journal of Industrial Medicine*, 46, 593–596.

13. Lanphear, B. P., et al. (2005). Low-level environmental lead exposure and children's intellectual function: An international pooled analysis. *Environmental Health Perspectives*, 113: 894–899; Bellinger, D. C. (2004). What is an adverse effect? A possible resolution of clinical and epidemiological perspectives on neurobehavioural toxicity. *Environmental Research*, 95, 395–405.

14. Tilson, H. A. (2000). Neurotoxicology risk assessment guidelines: Developmental neurotoxicity of environmental agents in the neonate. *Neurotoxicology*, 21, 189–194; Eriksson, P. (1997). Developmental neurotoxicity of environmental agents in the neonate. *Neurotoxicology*, 18, 719–726.

15. Claudio, L., et al. (2000). Testing methods for developmental neurotoxicity of environmental chemicals. *Toxicology and Applied Pharmacology*, 164, 1–14.

16. Gibson, J. L. (1904). A plea for painted railing and painted walls of rooms as the source of lead poisoning among Queensland children. *Australasian Medical Gazette*, 23, 149–153.

17. Byers, R. K., and Lord, E. E. (1943). Late effect of lead poisoning on mental development. *American Journal of Diseases of Children*, 66, 471–494.

18. Landrigan, P. J., et al. (1975). Neuropsychological dysfunction in children with chronic low-level lead absorption. *Lancet*, 1, 708–712; Needleman, H. L., et al. (1979). Deficits in psychologic and classroom performance of children with elevated dentine lead levels. *New England Journal of Medicine*, 300, 689–695.

19. Winneke, G., et al. (1990). Results from the European multicenter study on lead neurotoxicity in children: Implications for risk assessment. *Neurotoxicology and Teratology*, 12, 553–559.

20. Landrigan, P. J. (2002). The worldwide problem of lead in petrol. *Bulletin of the World Health Organization*, 80, 768.

21. Lanphear, B. P., et al. (2005). *See* note 13.

22. Ibid.

23. Harada, M. (1995). Minamata disease: Methylmercury poisoning in Japan caused by environmental pollution. *Critical Reviews in Toxicology*, 25, 1–24.

24. Elhassani, S. B. (1982). The many faces of methylmercury poisoning. *Journal of Toxicology. Clinical Toxicology*, 19, 875–906; Pierce, P. E., et al. (1972). Alkyl mercury poisoning in humans. Report of an outbreak. *JAMA*, 220, 1439–1442.

25. Marsh, D. O., et al. (1981). Dose-response relationship for human fetal exposure to methylmercury. *Clinical Toxicology*, 18, 1311–1318.

26. Kjesstrom, T., et al. (1989). Physical and mental development of children with prenatal exposure to mercury from fish. Stage 2, interviews and psychological tests at age 6. (Report 3642). Stockholm: National Swedish Environmental Protection Board.

27. Grandjean, P., et al. (1997). Cognitive deficit in 7-year-old children with prenatal exposure to methylmercury. *Neurotoxicology and Teratology*, 19, 417–428.

28. Myers, G. J., et al. (2003). Prenatal methylmercury exposure from ocean fish consumption in the Seychelles child development study. *Lancet*, 361, 1686–1692.

29. Grandjean, P., et al. (2005). Health effects and risk assessment. In *Dynamics of Mercury Pollution on Regional and Global Scales: Atmospheric Processes and Human Exposures around the World*, eds. N. Pirrone and K. R. Mahaffey. Norwell, MA: Springer, 499–523.

30. National Research Council. (2000). *Toxicological Effects of Methylmercury*. Washington: National Academy Press.

31. United Nations Environment Programme. (2002). *Global Mercury Assessment*. Geneva, Switzerland: United Nations Environment Programme.

32. Hviid, A., et al. (2003). Association between thimerosal-containing vaccine and autism. *JAMA, 290*, 1763–1766.

33. Yamashita, N., et al. (1972). Recent observations of Kyoto children poisoned by arsenic-tainted "Morinaga dry milk" [trans from Japanese]. *Nippon Eiseigaku Zasshi, 27*, 364–399.

34. Ohira, M., and Aoyama, H. (1973). Epidemiological studies on the Morinaga powdered milk poisoning incident [trans from Japanese]. *Nippon Eiseigaku Zasshi, 27*, 500–531.

35. Yamashita, N., et al. (1972). *See* note 33.

36. Tsai, S. Y., et al. (2003). The effects of chronic arsenic exposure from drinking water on the neurobehavioral development in adolescence. *Neurotoxicology, 24*, 747–753; Wasserman, G. A., et al. (2004). Water arsenic exposure and children's intellectual function in Araihazar, Bangladesh. *Environmental Health Perspectives, 112*, 1329–1333; Calderon, J., et al. (2001). Exposure to arsenic and lead and neuropsychological development in Mexican children. *Environmental Research, 85*, 69–76.

37. Smith, A. B., et al. (1982). Metabolic and health consequences of occupational exposure to polychlorinated biphenyls. *British Journal of Industrial Medicine, 39*, 361–369.

38. Guo, Y. L., et al. (2004). Health effects of prenatal exposure to polychlorinated biphenyls and dibenzofurans. *International Archives of Occupational and Environmental Health, 77*, 153–158.

39. Chen, Y. C. J., et al. (1992). Cognitive development of Yu-Chen [Oil Disease] in children prenatally exposed to heat-graded PCBs. *JAMA, 268*, 3213–3218.

40. Gladen, B. C., et al. (1990). Development after exposure to polychlorinated biphenyls and dichlorodiphenyl dichloroethene transplacentally and through human milk. *Journal of Pediatrics, 116*, 38–45; Jacobson, J. L., Jacobson, S. W., and Humphrey, H. E. B. (1990). Effect of in utero exposure to polychlorinated biphenyls and related contaminants on cognitive functioning in young children. *Journal of Pediatrics, 116*, 38–45; Jacobson, J. L., and Jacobson, S. W. (1996). Intellectual impairment in children exposed to polychlorinated biphenyls in utero. *New England Journal of Medicine, 335*, 783–789.

41. Vreugdenhil, H. J., et al. (2004). Effects of perinatal exposure to PCBs on neuropsychological functions in the Rotterdam cohort at 9 years of age. *Neuropsychology, 18*, 185–193; Walkowiak, J., et al. (2001). Environmental exposure to polychlorinated biphenyls and quality of home environment: Effects on psychodevelopment in early childhood. *Lancet, 358*, 1602–1607.

42. European Food Safety Authority. (2006). Opinion of the CONTAM panel related to the presence of nondioxin-like polychlorinated biphenyls (PCB) in feed and food. http://www.efsa.euint/science/contam/contam_opinions/1229_en.html (accessed August 12, 2006).

43. Sokol, R. J., Delaney-Black, V., and Nordstrom, B. (2003). Fetal alcohol spectrum disorder. *Journal of the American Medical Association, 290*, 2996–2999; Streissguth, A. P., Barr, H. M., and Sampson, P. D. (1990). Moderate prenatal alcohol exposure: Effects on child IQ and learning problems at age $7\frac{1}{2}$ years. *Alcoholism, Clinical and Experimental Research, 14*, 662–669.

44. Hersh, J. H., et al. (1985). Toluene embryopathy. *Journal of Pediatrics, 106,* 922–927; Arnold, G. I., et al. (1994). Toluene embryopathy: Clinical delineation and developmental follow-up. *Pediatrics, 93,* 216–220; Pearson, M. A., et al. (1994). Toluene embryopathy: Delineation of the phenotype and comparison with fetal alcohol syndrome. *Pediatrics, 93,* 211–215.

45. Kimbrough, R. D., et al. (1989). *Clinical Effects of Environmental Chemicals: A Software Approach to Etiologic Diagnosis.* New York: Hemisphere.

46. Guillette, E. A., et al. (1998). An anthropological approach to the evaluation of preschool children exposed to pesticides in Mexico. *Environmental Health Perspectives, 106,* 347–353.

47. Rohlman, D. S., et al. (2005). Neurobehavioral performance in preschool children from agricultural and non-agricultural communities in Oregon and North Carolina. *Neurotoxicology, 26,* 589–598.

48. Grandjean, P., et al. (2006). Pesticide exposure and stunting as independent predictors of neurobehavioral deficits in Ecuadorian school children. *Pediatrics, 117,* 546–556.

49. Ruckart, P. Z., et al. (2004). Long-term neurobehavioral health effects of methyl parathion exposure in children in Mississippi and Ohio. *Environmental Health Perspectives, 112,* 46–51; Young, J. G., et al. (2005). Association between in utero organophosphate pesticide exposure and abnormal reflexes in neonates. *Neurotoxicology, 26,* 199–209; Berkowitz, G. S., et al. (2004). In utero pesticide exposure, maternal paraxonase activity, and head circumference. *Environmental Health Perspectives, 112,* 1125–1132; Whyatt, R. M., et al. (2004). Prenatal insecticide exposures and birth weight and length among an urban minority cohort. *Environmental Health Perspectives, 112,* 1125–1132.

50. Pal, P. K., Samii, A., and Calne, D. B. (1999). Manganese neurotoxicity: A review of clinical features, imaging, and pathology. *Neurotoxicology, 20,* 227–238.

51. Takser, L., et al. (1999). Manganese, monamine metabolite levels at birth, and child psychomotor development. *Neurotoxicology, 20,* 327–342.

52. Wright, R. O., et al. (2006). Neuropsychological correlates of hair arsenic, manganese, and cadmium level in school-age children residing near a hazardous waste site. *Neurotoxicology, 27,* 210–216; Wasserman, G. A., et al. (2006). Water manganese exposure and children's intellectual function in Araihazar, Bangladesh. *Environmental Health Perspectives, 114,* 124–129.

53. Xiang, Q., et al. (2003). Effect of fluoride in drinking water on children's intelligence. *Fluoride, 36,* 84–94; Lu, Y., et al. (2000). Effect of high-fluoride water on intelligence in children. *Fluoride, 33,* 74–78.

54. Qin, L. S., and Cui, S. Y. (1990). The influence of drinking water fluoride on pupils' IQ as measured by Rui Wen's standard [in Chinese]. *Chinese Journal of the Control of Epidemiological Disease, 5,* 203–204.

55. National Research Council. (2005). *Health Implications of Perchlorate Ingestion.* Washington, DC: National Academy Press.

56. Rodier, P. M. (1995). *See* note 4; Takser, I., et al. (2005). Thyroid hormones in pregnancy in relation to environmental exposure to organochlorine compounds and mercury. *Environmental Health Perspectives, 113,* 1039–1045; Grandjean, P. (1991). Effects on reserve capacity: Significance for exposure limits. *Science of the Total Environment, 101,* 25–32.

57. Eddleston, M., et al. (2002). Pesticide poisoning in the developing world—a minimum pesticides list. *Lancet, 360,* 1163–1167.

58. U.S. Environmental Protection Agency. (1998). *Chemical Hazard Data Availability Study: What Do We Really Know about the Safety of High Production Volume Chemicals?* Washington, DC: Office of Pollution Prevention and Toxics.

59. Ibid.

60. Ibid.

61. Goldey, E. S., Tilson, H. A., and Crofton, K. M. (1995). Implications of the use of neonatal birth weight, growth, viability, and survival data for predicting developmental neurotoxicity: A survey of the literature. *Neurotoxicology and Teratology,* 17, 313–323; Hass, U. (2003). Current status of developmental neurotoxicity: Regulatory view. *Toxicology Letters,* 140–141, 155–159.

62. Ibid.

63. Rice, D., and Barone, S., Jr. (2000). *See* note 4; Tilson, H. A. (2000). *See* note 14; Eriksson, P. (1997). *See* note 14.

64. Kogevinas, M., Andersen, A. M., and Oldsen, J. (2004). Collaboration is needed to co-ordinate European birth cohort studies. *International Journal of Epidemiology,* 33: 1172–1173.

65. Grandjean, P. (2004). Implications of the precautionary principle for primary prevention and research. *Annual Review of Public Health,* 25, 199–223.

Index

About the Editor and Contributors

EDITOR

SHARNA OLFMAN is a professor of clinical and developmental psychology at Point Park University, the founding director of the Childhood and Society Symposium, and the editor of the Childhood in America book series for Praeger Publishers. Her books include *Child Honoring: How to Turn This World Around* (coedited with Raffi Cavoukian, 2006), *No Child Left Different* (2006), *Childhood Lost* (2005), and *All Work and No Play: How Educational Reforms Are Harming Our Preschoolers* (2003). Dr. Olfman is a member of the Council of Human Development, and is a partner in the Alliance for Childhood. She has written and lectured widely on the subjects of gender development, women's mental health, infant care, and child psychopathology.

CONTRIBUTORS

DANIEL BURSTON chairs the Department of Psychology at Duquesne University and is the author of several books, including *Erik Erikson and the American Psyche: Ego, Ethics and Evolution*, *The Wing of Madness: The Life and Work of R. D. Laing*, and *The Legacy of Erich Fromm*. He is an associate at the Center for the Philosophy of Science at the University of Pittsburgh, and serves on the editorial boards of the *Journal of the Society for Existential Analysis*, the *Journal of Humanistic Psychology*, and *Janus Head*.

LAWRENCE DILLER is a behavioral/developmental pediatrician and family therapist. He has evaluated and treated more than 2,500 children and their families over the past twenty-nine years. Dr. Diller's practice is based in the San Francisco Bay Area suburb of Walnut Creek, and he lives nearby in the town of Piedmont with his wife and two teenage sons. He is an assistant clinical professor of pediatrics at the University of California, San Francisco. He has written many articles on children's behavior and psychiatric medication for both professional and lay literature that have drawn national and international notice. His book *Running on Ritalin: A Physician Reflects on Children, Society, and Performance in a Pill*, published in 1998, was featured in a *Time* magazine cover story on Ritalin. His second book, *Should I Medicate My Child? Sane Solutions for Troubled Kids with—and without—Medication*, was published in 2002. Dr. Diller has appeared many times on national television and radio shows, including *Nightline*, PBS's *NewsHour*, *Good Morning America*, CBS's *Early Morning*, the *Today Show*, *Frontline*, and NPR's *Fresh Air*. His two-part Kids on Drugs series, featured in the online magazine *Salon.com*, won the Society of Professional Journalists' Excellence in Journalism award in 2000. He provided expert testimony on Ritalin before a committee of Congress in May 2000, and to the President's Council on Bioethics in December 2002. His latest book, *The Last Normal Child: Essays on the Intersection of Kids, Culture, and Psychiatric Drugs*, was released in September 2006.

DAVID HEALY is a professor of psychiatry at Cardiff University. He studied medicine at University College Dublin, Ireland, and at Cambridge University. He is a former Secretary of the British Association for Psychopharmacology, and is author of more than 140 peer-reviewed articles and 15 books, including *The Antidepressant Era, The Creation of Psychopharmacology, The Psychopharmacologists* (3 vols), and *Let Them Eat Prozac*.

Dr. Healy's main areas of research are clinical trials and psychopharmacology. He has testified as an expert witness in murder and suicide trials involving psychotropic drugs, and has brought problems with these drugs to the attention of U.S. and British regulators, raising awareness of how pharmaceutical companies sell drugs by marketing diseases and co-opting academic opinion-leaders, ghostwriting their articles.

TONI VAUGHN HEINEMAN is the founder and executive director of A Home Within, currently the only national organization to focus exclusively on meeting the emotional needs of current and former foster children. Through A Home Within, clinicians in private practice offer on a pro bono basis weekly psychotherapy sessions "for as long as it takes" to help each client. Clinicians at A Home Within work from the premise that all children need at least one stable, caring adult to thrive, and that the therapeutic relationship helps children build other relationships to support and sustain them. Dr. Heineman is the author of *The Abused Child: Psychodynamic Understanding and Treatment*, and the coeditor of *Building A Home Within: Meeting the Emotional Needs of Children and Youth in Foster Care*. She has presented numerous workshops to social workers, psychologists, foster parents, and youths.

PHILIP J. LANDRIGAN chairs the Department of Community and Preventive Medicine at the Mount Sinai School of Medicine in New York City, where he also teaches as the Ethel H. Wise Professor. Dr. Landrigan earned his medical degree at Harvard in 1967. From 1970 to 1985, Dr. Landrigan served in the U.S. Public Health Service as an Epidemic Intelligence Service Officer, and as medical epidemiologist for the Centers for Disease Control. He has been at the Mount Sinai School of Medicine since 1985.

Dr. Landrigan is a member of the Institute of Medicine of the National Academy of Sciences. At the National Academy of Sciences he chaired the Committee on Environmental Neurotoxicology and Committee on Pesticides in the Diets of Infants and Children. The report on pesticides and children's health was instrumental in securing passage of the Food Quality Protection Act of 1996, the major federal pesticide law in the United States. From 1995 to 1997, Dr. Landrigan served on the Presidential Advisory Committee on Gulf War Veterans' Illnesses. In 1997 and 1998, Dr. Landrigan served as Senior Advisor on Children's Health to the Administrator of the U.S. Environmental Protection Agency (EPA), and was instrumental in helping to establish the Office of Children's Health Protection at the EPA.

JOANNA LE NOURY is a psychologist who earned her doctorate at Leeds University, where she studied aspects of behavior and nutrition. She has since served as a research officer, first at Bangor University and more recently at the North Wales Department of Psychiatry, where she has studied the impact of nutrition on serious mental illness and the influence of cognitive function on mood disorder.

ELIZABETH J. ROBERTS is a child and adolescent psychiatrist, and author of *Should You Medicate Your Child's Mind? A Child Psychiatrist Makes Sense of Whether to Give Kids Meds*. Dr. Roberts is the medical director of a psychiatric emergency room for children in Southern California, medical director at Casa de Lago, a residential eating disorder treatment center for adolescent girls, and maintains a private practice. Her guidance of children has encompassed myriad pursuits and spanned more than thirty years. Dr. Roberts has raised three children, taught kindergarten classes through twelfth grade in both public and private schools, and has practiced child psychiatry in a number of settings, including hospitals, clinics, and drug rehabilitation programs such as the Hazelden teen unit outside Chicago. Dr. Roberts has appeared on a number of television programs—the *Oprah Show* and *ABC News* among them—and has been a guest on numerous radio shows—the *Milt Rosenberg Show* in Chicago, the *Pete Wilson Show* in San Francisco, *Positive Parenting*, the *Good Parenting Show,* and nationally syndicated programs on the Radio America Network, to name a few. Her opinion piece exposing children's overmedication with psychiatric drugs was published in the *Washington Post*. She has been quoted in the *Chicago Tribune, Chicago Sun Times,* and the *New York City Parent Guide*. Dr. Roberts has lectured at the University of California at Berkeley on the use of psychiatric medications in children. She has conducted public seminars on this subject and on effective parenting and recognizing mental illness in children to audiences at hospitals, high schools, and meetings of Children and Adults with Attention Deficit Disorder (ChADD). More information can be found at her Web site, www.DrElizabethRoberts.com.

WILLIAM J. PURCELL is a clinical psychologist and the co-founder of Children's Charter, a treatment and advocacy center for children and families in Waltham, Massachusetts. As a forensic expert, he has specialized in intensive diagnostic procedures to assess the needs of children and families in complex and disputed situations. He frequently testifies in probate and family courts and often represents children's interests to the courts as a guardian ad litem. He is currently an associate professor in psychology and chairs the Department of Humanities and Human Sciences at Point Park University.

ROBERT WHITAKER is the author of *Mad in America: Bad Science, Bad Medicine, and the Enduring Mistreatment of the Mentally Ill*. His articles on the drug industry and the mentally ill have won several awards, including the George Polk Award for medical writing, and an award from the National Association of Science Writers for best magazine article. A series he cowrote for the *Boston Globe* was named a finalist for the Pulitzer Prize.